D1446548

PROVERBS:

UNCOMMON SENSE

Connect with God. Connect with others.
Connect with life.

Proverbs: Uncommon Sense
Youth Edition Leader Book
© 2006 Serendipity
Reprinted 2007, 2009, 2011, 2012, 2013

Published by LifeWay Press®
Nashville, Tennessee

ISBN: 978-1-5749-4285-9
Item 001303840

Dewey Decimal Classification: 223.7
Subject Headings:
BIBLE. O.T. PROVERBS—STUDY \ CHRISTIAN LIFE

Printed in the United States of America

Student Ministry Publishing
LifeWay Church Resources
One LifeWay Plaza
Nashville, TN 37234-0144

We believe that the Bible has God for its author; salvation for its end; and truth, without any mixture of
error, for its matter and that all Scripture is totally true and trustworthy. The 2000 statement of
The Baptist Faith and Message is our doctrinal guideline.

CONTENTS

 **EXPERIENCE**

Combine *teaching that engages a large-group* with dynamic *small-group experiences and discussions* and the result is students grappling with reality and real life change. Throughout 13 sessions, small groups will find power in just being together in community. Help them connect with God ... connect with each other ... connect with life! Each session consists of a four-part agenda. In addition, "Get Ready" and "Now What?" segments enable students to dig a little deeper and give God more opportunity to impact their lives.

 Get Ready

To get the most from this experience, students should spend time with God each day leading up to the session. They simply wrap their brains around the short Bible passages, listen to God, and jot down thoughts and insights.

 So What?

The master-teacher will lead the entire group in understanding what God has to say on the topic. Content has biblical depth, yet is engaging. Students can follow along, jot notes, and respond to questions in their student books.

 LifePoint

Welcome and communicate the "LifePoint" or big idea for the session, and then divide students into small groups. NOTE: If feasible, keep the same groups together each week to enhance the depth of group dynamic and potential for life change.

 Do What?

All study should direct us toward action and life change. The goal in small groups is to be real with each other in order to connect with God, with others, and with life. Students will find power to integrate truth into life with the support and prayers of other students.

 Say What?

Small-group facilitators lead students in interactive experiences and discussions. "Random Question of the Week" helps students open up and encourages them to join activities or discussions that lead into the session topic.

 Now What?

To see real power in life, encourage students not to just leave the session and go on with life as normal. The "Now What?" assignments help them continue their journeys and give them opportunity to go deeper with God.

LIFE CONNECTIONS® YOUTH

AT A GLANCE

Get Ready — Daily time with God & your journal

LifePoint	Large Group: Welcome & Theme	
Say What?	Small Group: Fun & Interaction	
So What?	Large Group: Teaching & Discovery (Master Teacher)	
Do What?	Small Group: Getting Real & Connecting	

Now What? — Continue your journey...

LEADERS AND FACILITATORS

Every Life Connections group must fill three important roles. Each responsibility is vital to the success of the class.

Teacher—The teacher is the key leader of any Life Connections group.
It is the responsibility of the teacher to:
1. enlist facilitators and apprentices.
2. make facilitators and apprentices aware of their roles and be certain these responsibilities are carried out.
3. meet periodically with facilitators to train, encourage, and inspire them.
4. cast vision for and keep the group focused on the goals of the group.
5. guide group members to understand and commit to the group covenant.
6. be sure the group utilizes, fills, and evangelizes through use of the empty chair concept.
7. act as the Master Teacher for the group.
8. keep the group on task throughout each session.

Facilitator—Each subgroup will have a facilitator. It is the responsibility of the facilitators to:
1. lead each individual in the subgroup in "Say What?" activities.
2. guide those in the subgroup to commit to apply the lessons learned in the "Do What?" section of the weekly session.
3. with sensitivity and wisdom, lead their subgroup to support one another during the "Do What?" closing and involve the subgroup in ministry and evangelism.
4. encourage students to go deeper by completing the "Get Ready" and "Now What?" times on their own between sessions.
5. minister to the needs of the subgroup members and lead them to minister to the needs of one another both during and between meetings.

Apprentice—Every subgroup must have an apprentice. When the group consistently has eight or more in attendance, the group should divide into two groups. The apprentice will become the facilitator of the new group and choose an apprentice who will someday be the facilitator of a group. It is the role of the apprentice to:
1. learn from the facilitator of the group.
2. make welcome all new subgroup members.
3. be certain student books and pens or pencils, and other supplies are available for all students.
4. turn in prayer requests.
5. encourage participation by actively participating themselves.
6. lead the group when the facilitator is unavailable.

CORE VALUES

Community:
God is relational, so He created us to live in relationship with Him and each other. Authentic community involves sharing life together and connecting on many levels with the people in our group.

Group Process:
Developing authentic community requires a step-by-step process. It's a journey of sharing our stories with each other and learning together.

Interactive Bible Study:
God provided the Bible as an instruction manual of life. We need to deepen our understanding of God's Word. People learn and remember more as they wrestle with truth and learn from others. The process of Bible discovery and group interaction will enhance our growth.

Experiential Growth:
The goal of studying the Bible together is not merely a quest for knowledge; this should result in real life change. Beyond solely reading, studying, and dissecting the Bible, being a disciple of Christ involves reunifying knowledge with experience. We do this by bringing our questions to God, opening a dialogue with our hearts (instead of killing our desires), and utilizing other ways to listen to God speak to us (group interaction, nature, art, movies, circumstances, and so on). Experiential growth is always grounded in the Bible as God's primary means of revelation and our ultimate truth-source.

The Power of God:
Our processes and strategies will be ineffective unless we invite and embrace God's presence and power. In order to experience community and growth, Jesus must be the centerpiece of our group experiences and the Holy Spirit must be at work.

Redemptive Community:
Healing best happens within the context of community and in relationship. A key aspect of our spiritual development is seeing ourselves through the eyes of others, sharing our stories, and ultimately being set free from the secrets and the lies we embrace that enslave our souls.

Mission:
God has invited us into a larger story with a great mission. It is a mission that involves setting captives free and healing the broken-hearted (Isa. 61:1-2). However, we can only join in this mission to the degree that we've let Jesus bind up our wounds and set us free. As a group experiences true redemptive community, other people will be attracted to that group, and through that group to Jesus. We should be alert to inviting others while we maintain (and continue to fill) an "empty chair" in our meetings to remind us of others who need to encounter God and authentic Christian community.

GROUP COVENANT

It is important that your group covenant together, agreeing to live out important group values. Once these values are agreed upon, your group will be on its way to experiencing true Christian community. It's very important that your group discuss these values—preferably as you begin this study. The first session would be most appropriate. (Check the rules to which each member of your group agrees.)

☐ Priority: While you are in this course of study, you give the group meetings priority.

☐ Participation: Everyone is encouraged to participate and no one dominates.

☐ Respect: Everyone is given the right to his or her own opinion, and all questions are encouraged and respected.

☐ Confidentiality: Anything that is said in the meeting is never repeated outside the meeting without permission. *Note: Church staff may be required by law to report illegal activities.*

☐ Life Change: We will regularly assess our own progress in applying *LifePoints* and encourage one another in our pursuit of becoming more like Christ.

☐ Care and Support: Permission is given to call upon each other at any time, especially in times of crisis. The group will provide care for every member.

☐ Accountability: We agree to let the members of the group hold us accountable to the commitments we make in whatever loving ways we decide upon. Unsolicited advice giving is not permitted.

☐ Empty Chair: The group is open to welcoming new people at every meeting.

☐ Mission: We agree as a group to reach out and invite others to join us.

☐ Ministry: We will encourage one another to volunteer and serve in a ministry and to support missions by giving financially and/or personally serving.

Session

1

WISDOM: LEARNIG TO LIVE LIFE WITH SKILL

Connections Prep

MAIN LIFEPOINT:

Wisdom is a skill that is learned throughout life. However, contrary to popular belief, wisdom does not refer to knowledge or intelligence.

To reinforce the LifePoint, leaders and small-group facilitators should understand the following more detailed CheckPoints and "Do" Points.

BIBLE STUDY CHECKPOINTS:

· Understand the difference between knowledge, intelligence, and wisdom
· Examine the ways to capture wisdom
· Evaluate ways to lay a foundation of wisdom for your own life

LIFE CHANGE "DO" POINTS:

· Commit to discover wise people
· Search for wisdom in God's Word
· Develop a healthy fear of the Lord

PREPARATION:

☐ Review the leader book for this session and prepare your teaching.
☐ Determine how you will subdivide students into small discussion groups.
☐ Recruit mature students or adults as small-group facilitators. Be sure these facilitators plan to attend.

REQUIRED SUPPLIES:

☐ *Proverbs: Uncommon Sense* leader books for each group facilitator
☐ *Proverbs: Uncommon Sense* student books for each student
☐ Pens or pencils for each student

This "Get Ready" section is primarily for the students, but leaders and facilitators will benefit from these devotionals as well.

 **Get Ready**

Read one of these short Bible passages each day and spend a few minutes wrapping your brain around it. Be sure to jot down any insights you discover.

MONDAY

Read Proverbs 1:1-6.

Have you ever made unwise choices? What would you say were the results of your unwise choices? How have unwise choices affected you spiritually?

TUESDAY

Read Proverbs 1:7, 9:10-12.

Have you ever made unwise choices? What would you say were the results of your unwise choices? How have unwise choices affected you spiritually?

WEDNESDAY

Read Proverbs 2:1-5.

What is something you practice doing? Why do you spend time practicing? How can you spend time searching for wisdom? Why should you search for wisdom?

THURSDAY

Read Proverbs 3:5-6.

What does it mean to "Trust in the Lord"? Have you ever been tempted to follow wisdom from someone other than God?

FRIDAY

Read Proverbs 3:7-8.

What is the difference between having wisdom in your own eyes and having wisdom in God's eyes? Which is better? Why?

SATURDAY

Read Proverbs 3:25-26.

What figurative snares, traps, have caught you? What snares in life have you been able to avoid? Was it easier to be trapped or to avoid being trapped? Explain.

SUNDAY

Read Matthew 7:24-27.

What is the difference between a house that is built on the rock and a house that is built on the sand? Spiritually, how can you learn the difference between a "rock" and "sand"? Are you building your house on the rock or the sand?

LARGE-GROUP OPENING:
Get everyone's attention. Make announcements. Open your session with a prayer. Read the LifePoint to the students.

 LifePoint

Wisdom is a skill that is learned throughout life. However, contrary to popular belief, wisdom does not refer to knowledge or intelligence.

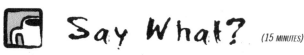

Say What? *(15 MINUTES)*

Random Question of the Week:

When was the last time you had a milk moustache?

Group Experience: Puzzling Questions

Share the following "Wisdom" questions with the students in your small group, but do not supply the answers right away. Have students work together to answer the questions. If possible, give the students clues so they can discover the answers to each question on their own. Occasionally lead the group astray by hinting in the wrong direction. Allow the students the opportunity to try to find the answers using their own logic.

1. Two sons and two fathers go fishing. They each catch one fish. The total number of fish they catch is three. How is this possible?

Answer: The men involved are a grandfather, a father, and a son. The father is a son to the grandfather and a father to the son.

2. A man comes home one day and begins to check his e-mail when he discovers Myrtle lying on the floor, dead. There is broken glass and a large quantity of water on the floor. What happened?

Answer: Myrtle is a fish. The broken glass is the fish bowl.

3. You have two traditional hourglass timers. One is a 7-minute timer and the other is an 11-minute timer. You want to boil an ostrich egg for exactly 15 minutes. How do you do it? How soon after the start of the whole process will the egg be ready?

After the exercise, answer these follow-up questions:

1. How did these questions make you feel?

2. Do you have to resist giving up when the questions are difficult?

Answer: Start both timers together. When the 7-minute timer finishes, turn it over immediately. It will run for 4 minutes before the 11-minute timer finishes. Turn the 7-minute timer over again at that point, and it will measure 4 more minutes: 15 minutes total.

3. How did you feel when you received advice that didn't help you answer the questions?

4. Finish this sentence: The best advice ever given to me was . . .

 So What? *(30 MINUTES)*

Teaching Outline

I. A Wise Request
A. Wisdom defined
B. We learn a lot just from living life—that's wisdom
C. Solomon, the wisest man ever, gained his wisdom by asking for it
D. Solomon sought wisdom because he wanted to be the best leader possible

II. Proverbs 1:1-7

III. Living with Skill
A. Proverbs encourages us as we live our lives
B. Proverbs is God's collection of wisdom
C. Intelligence, knowledge, and wisdom are different
    1. Intelligence is the ability to learn
    2. Knowledge is the information storehouse
    3. Wisdom is the understanding of life and how it works
D. Wisdom is gleaned both from what we are able to observe and what we are
    unable to observe

IV. The Value of Wisdom
A. Part of gaining wisdom is knowing how to recognize it
B. Wise people have always been valued
C. Wise individuals gain, learn, understand, received, listen, and
    increase knowledge

V. Laying the Foundation
A. Fear of the Lord is the beginning of wisdom
B. A person can be wise in many ways
C. Fearing the Lord is not old fashioned, it's real
D. There are benefits to diligent work

**TEACHING FOR THE
LARGE GROUP**

❶ **What is the
definition of wisdom?**

❷ **How did Solomon
become wise?**

Before the session,
enlist a student to read
Proverbs 1:1-7.

A Wise Request

You can choose to live life hoping things work out for you, or you can choose to live life with skill. The "skill" required to live life correctly is called wisdom. ❶ <u>Wisdom is defined as, "The ability to discern or judge what is true, right, or lasting; insight."</u> (*The American Heritage® Dictionary of the English Language, Fourth Edition Copyright © 2000 by Houghton Mifflin Company.*) We learn to live life and gain insight through the simple act of living! Sounds easy, but it is anything but easy. Many times we don't learn from our mistakes. Also, we often recognize other's mistakes but don't see the same traps when we fall into them ourselves. Can you relate?

We can learn quite a bit about wisdom from someone the Bible refers to as the wisest man ever—King Solomon (1 Kings 3:12). King Solomon was an extremely wise man. ❷ <u>He gained his wisdom by asking God for it.</u> Solomon had the opportunity to ask God for anything he wanted—he had the opportunity to get whatever he wanted—and of all the things he could have asked for he asked for wisdom. He didn't ask for beauty, a faster horse than his neighbor, or money; he asked for wisdom. Solomon wanted wisdom because he wanted to be a wise ruler for God's people. Solomon was uncomfortable with the level of wisdom he had on his own, and he wanted to be faithful to the God who had appointed Him as King of Israel.

Learning from the Bible

¹ The proverbs of Solomon son of David, king of Israel:
² For gaining wisdom and being instructed;
for understanding insightful sayings;
³ for receiving wise instruction
in righteousness, justice, and integrity;
⁴ for teaching shrewdness to the inexperienced,
knowledge and discretion to a young man—
⁵ a wise man will listen and increase his learning,
and a discerning man will obtain
guidance—
⁶ for understanding a proverb or a parable,
the words of the wise, and their riddles.
⁷ The fear of the LORD
is the beginning of knowledge;
fools despise wisdom and instruction.—Proverbs 1:1-7

Learning to Live Life with Skill . . . WISDOM

Proverbs was written for everyone. ❸ The book was written to encourage the simple and inexperienced (v. 4) as well as the wise and the discerning (v. 5). The purpose of the book is to help people gain wisdom and learn how to live life with skill. God is behind the words Solomon wrote; He directed him from behind the scenes. The book of Proverbs is God's collection of wisdom for us.

❹ A lot of people don't know the difference between intelligence, knowledge, and wisdom. ❺ Intelligence is the ability to learn. There are different kinds of intelligence just like there are different kinds of learning styles. ❻ Knowledge is the information storehouse of facts, memories, and experiences that we can recall. These may include knowledge of wisdom principles, but this knowledge is not wisdom. Wisdom is not the same as intelligence or knowledge. ❼ It is a skill at living life that is arrived at by understanding how life works. Wisdom comes from two sources: observation and divine inspiration.

❽ A lot of wisdom can be gained from just paying attention in life. Popular proverbs often reflect this kind of wisdom. "Crime doesn't pay" reflects wisdom that comes simply from observation as does, "The early bird gets the worm." But some wisdom goes beyond what we can observe. This wisdom is given to us by God's perfect knowledge of His creation. For example, in Proverbs 6:16-19 Solomon tells us about six things the Lord hates and seven that are detestable to Him. Another example can be found in Proverbs 19:17 where God tells us, "Kindness to the poor is a loan to the LORD."

Learning the Value of Wisdom...

Part of gaining wisdom is learning how to recognize it. When you read Proverbs you might notice that wisdom doesn't just appear. It doesn't occur naturally. Wise people learn to be wise over time; they aren't born that way. Wise people have been highly valued throughout ancient history. Kings have consulted wise men looking for help and advice. Wise men were not necessarily the smartest men with the most knowledge; they were skilled in living life and dealing with people. Kings sought wise men's counsel because wise men had taken time to gain, learn, understand, receive, listen, and increase knowledge and obtain insight. ❾ The action verbs described in Proverbs 1:1-7 are gaining, being instructed, understanding, receiving, teaching, listening, increasing and obtaining.

Laying the Wisdom Foundation

⑩ What is true wisdom based on?

⑩ The fear of the Lord is the beginning of wisdom, not because it is basic or elementary, but because true wisdom is based on it. There is secular wisdom, but it is incomplete. Wisdom that is not based on the fear of God lacks depth that only the Lord can bring.

We can observe life and learn to act wisely in many ways. We can learn to avoid arguments, value friendships, choose words, and discipline children. Yet, a person who is wise in these ways but doesn't fear the Lord is missing a great deal. His wisdom is mostly about personal gain rather than respect for God.

⑪ True wisdom is associated only with God.

⑪ True wisdom is related to God: "The way of the Lord is a stronghold for the honorable, but destruction awaits the malicious" (Prov. 10:29). God is a fortress for those who fear Him. When we follow God's wisdom, we are protected from the natural consequences of folly, but if we have a relationship with Him, He also protects us from events we have no power over.

⑫ Why isn't the fear of the Lord an old-fashioned concept?

Some people think that fearing the Lord is an old-fashioned concept that isn't relevant for modern-day followers of Jesus. However, the fear of the Lord is not an old-fashioned concept because God does judge. Just because people get away with evil now doesn't mean they always will. Besides, fearing God involves a healthy fear; it is like fearing a good father who loves you but will discipline you to help you grow to responsible adulthood. **⑫** Even if we are confident that we have a relationship with God through Jesus Christ, we must still have a healthy fear of rebellion against the God who made us and saved us.

Proverbs calls us to fear God and live life by His wisdom. In order to do that, we clearly have to do some work. The book of Proverbs is full of examples of the benefits of that hard work. For instance, when we live life by God's wisdom, we will live lives that are more pleasing to our Father in heaven.

Do What? *(15 MINUTES)*

SMALL-GROUP TIME:
Use this time to help students begin to integrate the truth they've learned into their lives while they connect with other students in the group, the leaders, and with God.

After presenting the teaching material, ask students to divide back into small groups and discuss the "Do What?" questions. Small group facilitators should lead the discussions and set the tone by being open and honest in responding to each question.

Group Experience: Making It Personal

1. Does knowing King Solomon as the wisest man to ever live help you dig deeper into the Proverbs for wisdom? Why or why not?

2. How would you describe someone with a healthy fear of God?

3. Which area of your life causes you to struggle the most in regards to wisdom?
   - ☐ Learning from others' mistakes
   - ☐ Understanding and learning from my own mistakes
   - ☐ Spending time gaining knowledge from the Bible
   - ☐ Developing a healthy view of the "fear" of God
   - ☐ Not consciously trying to gain wisdom
   - ☐ Other:

4. Complete this sentence: In order to gain wisdom, I need to . . .

Small-group facilitators should reinforce the LifePoint for this session, make sure that student's questions are invited and addressed honestly.

LifePoint Review

Wisdom is a skill that is learned throughout life. However, contrary to popular belief, wisdom does not refer to knowledge or intelligence.

"Do" Points:

These "Do" Points will help you grab hold of this week's LifePoint. Be open and honest as you answer the questions within your small group.

1. <u>Commit to discover wise people.</u> You become like the people that surround you. This isn't just a cute saying; it's true! Have you ever thought about the way you talk? Do you have an accent? Where did you get your accent? You take on the characteristics of the people around you.
Are you surrounding yourself with wise people who will encourage you to fill your life with wisdom?

2. <u>Search for wisdom in God's Word</u>. The Bible is full of proverbs that give us instructions about how we are to live our lives. We don't just read the Bible like we read a novel for our English class. The Bible sheds God's light onto our lives and reveals areas where we are in need of wisdom.
Have you spent time searching God's Word for wisdom lately?

3. <u>Develop a healthy fear of the Lord</u>. As you develop wisdom in your life, you will continually have the option to live your life for yourself or for God.
As you increase your wisdom, how can a healthy fear of the Lord be a positive thing?

Be sure to end your session by asking students to share prayer needs with one another, especially as they relate to issues brought up by today's session.

Encourage students to list prayer needs for others in their books so they can pray for one another during the week. Assign a student coordinator in each small group to gather the group's requests and e-mail them to the group members.

Prayer Connection:

This is the time to encourage, support, and pray for each other in our journeys to grasp who God really is and how much He cares for each of us.

Share prayer needs with the group, especially those related to knowing and connecting with God. Your group facilitator will close your time in prayer.

Prayer Needs:

now What?

Encourage students to dig a little deeper by completing a "Now What?" assignment before the next time you meet. Remind students about the "Get Ready" short daily Bible readings and related questions at the beginning of session 2.

Deepen your understanding of who God is, and continue the journey you've begun today by choosing one of the following assignments to complete this week:

Option 1:

If you enjoy writing, take the time this week to write down any wise actions that you notice. Spend time searching for wisdom. When you notice wisdom occurring around you, take the time to write down what you see. Be prepared to share your observations next week with your small group.

Option 2:

Take some time this week to re-write Proverbs 1:1-7 in your own words. Feel free to paraphrase the passage or rewrite it in paragraph form. The important thing is to grasp and communicate the meaning of the passage. Then find a photograph from a magazine or newspaper or even your favorite web site that reminds you of this Scripture. Be prepared to share your thoughts next week with your small group.

Bible Reference Notes

Use these notes to deepen your understanding as you study the Bible on your own:

Proverbs 1:2 — *gaining wisdom.* The main theme in Proverbs is wisdom, the nature of it and how to obtain it. The proverbs are common-sense guidelines for living. They teach that fearing the Lord is the beginning of wisdom (v. 7).

Proverbs 1:3 — *wise instruction.* This is training in everyday actions, attitudes, and character that will lead to true success in life.

Proverbs 1:7 — *fear of the LORD* The fear of the Lord involves acknowledging God's power and sovereignty, then offering our obedience in light of it. The fool disregards God's presence and power, acting as if personal satisfaction is all that matters.

Proverbs 2:1-3 — The writer repeatedly appeals to his son to live a life of wisdom.

Proverbs 2:4 — *seek . . . treasure.* This is an apt comparison. To find treasure one must search, dig, and excavate. Finding wisdom requires similar activity.

Proverbs 2:5 — *then you will understand.* When we search for wisdom, we find God Himself, and our relationship with Him deepens.

Proverbs 3:5 — *with all your heart.* The Bible uses this phrase to express total commitment. The "Shema" in Deuteronomy 6:5 calls us to love God with all our hearts, minds, and souls. Jesus described this as the first and greatest commandment.

Proverbs 3:6 — *guide . . . paths.* This implies more than guidance. It means God intentionally removes obstacles from our path.

Session

2

STICKS AND STONES AND...
WORDS: THEY ALL HURT

Connections Prep

MAIN LIFEPOINT: The words we say have a lasting impact. When we speak without thinking or gossip about others, we are hurting—not helping—others.

To reinforce the LifePoint, leaders and small-group facilitators should understand the following more detailed CheckPoints and "Do" Points.

BIBLE STUDY CHECKPOINTS:
· Discover the power of words
· Examine the characteristics of foolish and destructive words
· Learn how to use words to heal, not to hurt

LIFE CHANGE "DO" POINTS:
· Commit to pay attention to your words
· Notice people who need encouragement
· Be on the lookout for flattery and gossip

PREPARATION:
☐ Review the leader book for this session and prepare your teaching.
☐ Determine how you will subdivide students into small discussion groups.
☐ Recruit mature students or adults as small-group facilitators. Be sure these facilitators plan to attend.

REQUIRED SUPPLIES:
☐ *Proverbs: Uncommon Sense* leader books for each group facilitator
☐ *Proverbs: Uncommon Sense* student books for each student
☐ Pens or pencils for each student
☐ A piece of paper and scissors for each student

 Get Ready

Read one of these short Bible passages each day and spend a few minutes wrapping your brain around it. Be sure to jot down any insights you discover.

MONDAY   **Read Proverbs 12:14; 13:3; 18:21.**
How important is your mouth? What makes your words so important to you? What "fruits" are coming from your mouth?

TUESDAY   **Read Proverbs 18:2,13.**
How important is it to listen to others? Which is harder for you—to listen to other people's thoughts or to share your own? Why?

WEDNESDAY   **Read Proverbs 18:8.**
What makes gossip so satisfying? Why do we gossip about others? How does spreading gossip about others make us feel about ourselves?

THURSDAY   **Read Proverbs 12:18.**
Journal in the space provided about a time when someone's reckless words hurt you. Pray for that person.

FRIDAY

Read Proverbs 21:23.

List ways you can guard your tongue. What is calamity?

SATURDAY

Read Proverbs 29:5.

What is flattery? Is it good or bad? Why?

2

SUNDAY

Read James 3:3-8.

How can your tongue influence the way others think of you? What areas of your speech do you struggle with?

LARGE-GROUP OPENING:
Get everyone's attention. Make announcements. Open your session with a prayer. Read the LifePoint to the students.

Ask the group about the "Now What?" activities from last week. If anyone brought a photograph from Option 2, give her time to show it.

 LifePoint

The words we say have a lasting impact. When we speak without thinking or gossip about others, we are hurting—not helping—others.

SMALL-GROUP TIME:
Instruct students to separate into smaller groups of 4-8, preferably in a circle configuration. Call on the mature student or adult leaders you recruited previously to facilitate each small group through this "Say What?" segment.

Say What? *(15 MINUTES)*

Random Question of the Week:

If you could meet one superhero (movie or cartoon), who would you meet and why?

Group Experience: Silent Simon Says

"Silent Simon Says" is just that—Simon Says with no talking. You will have to develop a sign for "Simon says" and students will have to be able to know when "Simon" is really talking. Create secret signs for several different actions. These may include "jump up and down," "spin in a circle," "hop like a frog," "raise your arms," and "take a step forward." Once everyone is comfortable you might try combining these commands.

Make sure you have clued in your leaders to all the secret signs. Also, be sure the leaders know the sign for "Simon says" so you can communicate with them—the sign should be rather simple to decode, but not obvious. You may choose to have a secret sign for your leaders that cues them to laugh. This will be a sign for them to laugh loudly and boisterously at your cue. This makes students aware that you have a system, and they must learn it.

Introduce the activity by saying only that during the game you will not be using any words. This can lead to some humor, some competitiveness, and maybe even a little frustration. Be ready for all emotions. Ask the leaders to be ready to eliminate anyone who makes a mistake.

Begin by doing your best to give the group wordless instructions. Play until you feel everyone understands what's going on. As you end your activity, ask students the following questions:

1. How did this activity make you feel?
2. What was the most frustrating part of this activity?
3. Have you ever been somewhere and been the only one who didn't know what was funny in a situation?
4. How important are words to you and your daily life?
5. Communication is important. If we can't communicate with others, we lose out on plenty of experiences. When someone knows something secret, we often get frustrated when they won't share it. How did you feel once you realized others knew the "secret sign" that allowed them to communicate with "Simon"?

Last week we studied about how to gain wisdom by learning to live life with skill. This week we will learn to apply that wisdom to our words as we discover that the things we say definitely affect others.

LARGE-GROUP TIME:
Have the students turn to face the front for this teaching time. Be sure you can make eye contact with each student in the room. Encourage students to follow along and take notes in their student books.

 # So What? *(30 MINUTES)*

2

Teaching Outline

I. The Power of Words
A. Words are probably the most important part of the communication process
B. We "write" many books with our words every week

II. Proverbs 12:14,18; 13:3; 18:2,8,13,21; 21:23; 29:5

III. Using Words to Heal
A. Choosing wise words is a common struggle
B. We grow relationships, primarily, through our words

IV. The Effects of Words
A. When we speak, we typically encourage or discourage
B. Words cannot be taken back once they have been let go
C. Foolish or sinful talk can be very damaging
D. There is fruit in wise words

V. Destructive Words
A. Rash words
B. Depression, resentment, and retaliation result from destructive words
C. Our words should encourage

VI. Speaking vs. Listening
A. Avoid "speaking out of turn"
B. A wise person listens and stores knowledge

VII. The Friend Separator
A. Gossip is a difficult temptation
B. Gossip takes joy or finds recreation in another's folly or pain
C. Gossip separates friends

Share the "So What?" teaching with your students. You may modify it to meet your needs.

Be sure to highlight the underlined information, which gives answers to the student book questions and fill-in-the-blanks (shown in the margins).

VIII. Poison Flattery
  A. Flattery is motivated by need or want
  B. Flattery is insincere
  C. Flattery is a trap

TEACHING FOR THE
LARGE GROUP

The Power of Words

❶ According to the old saying about "sticks and stones," what will never hurt us? Do you agree or disagree? Why?

Have you ever heard the expression, ❶ <u>"Sticks and stones can break my bones, but WORDS will never hurt me!"</u>? Do you believe that statement is true, or do you believe that words can be used as weapons just like a stick or a stone?

❷ Why would a person use words for the wrong reasons?

Words are all around us. Words are an important part of the human communication process. According to scientific studies, women use approximately 25,000 words per day, and men use about 12,000 words per day. If your every word was written, imagine how many books you would write in a week. So, throughout the course of your day you are sharing many words and communicating many things. Sometimes, though, we don't use our words for the right reasons. ❷ <u>We may use words that we don't really understand to try to impress others, or we may use our vast knowledge of words to confuse other people. Today we're going to focus on some passages from Proverbs that talk about the way we use our words.</u>

Before the session, enlist a student to read Proverbs 12:14,18; 13:3; 18:2,8,13,21; 21:23; 29:5.

Learning from the Bible

A man will be satisfied with good
by the words of his mouth,
and the work of a man's hands will reward him.—Proverbs 12:14

There is one who speaks rashly,
like a piercing sword;
but the tongue of the wise brings healing.—Proverbs 12:18

The one who guards his mouth protects his life;
the one who opens his lips invites his own ruin.—Proverbs 13:3

A fool does not delight in understanding,
but only wants to show off his opinions.—Proverbs 18:2

A gossip's words are like choice food
that goes down to one's innermost being.—Proverbs 18:8

LARGE-GROUP TIME CONTINUED:
This is the meat of the teaching time. Remind students to follow along and take notes in their student books.

As you share the "So What?" information with students, make it your own. Use your natural teaching style.

Emphasize <u>underlined information</u>, which gives answers to the student book questions or fill-in-the-blanks in the (shown in the margins).

❸ Give an example of how you can use words to develop and grow a relationship.

The one who gives an answer before he listens—
this is foolishness and disgrace for him.—Proverbs 18:13

Life and death are in the power of the tongue,
and those who love it will eat its fruit.—Proverbs 18:21

The one who guards his mouth and tongue
keeps himself out of trouble.—Proverbs 21:23

A man who flatters his neighbor
spreads a net for his feet.—Proverbs 29:5

2

Developing the Skill for Life—Using Words to Heal, Not Hurt

Choosing the words we use is an area of everyone's life that presents unique challenges. Our speech is extremely important to us. Think back over the past year. How many new people have you met and spoken to? How many relationships do you have apart from communication? Whether you use an audible voice or sign language, your words are an important part of your life. ❸ <u>Words are the primary way we develop and grow relationships with others. Whenever we begin a relationship, we use a greeting or an introduction. We build relationships by talking about common interests and sharing honest feelings. We repair relationships by speaking our apologies to someone we have offended.</u> Without words, we don't let people into our lives; we keep them at a distance.

Words and their Effects

We can use words very purposefully. When we speak, we are either encouraging or discouraging someone else. ❹ <u>According to Solomon, our words hold the key to life and death.</u> While our words might not literally kill someone, this thought wasn't hard to comprehend in Solomon's day. Think about it. Words cannot be taken back. We may apologize, yes, or cover our words up. But once they leave our mouths, they have been heard. We don't get a "do over" in the event of a mistake. This was especially true of Solomon. He lived in a day when the king's decision was final. When the king decided it was time for someone to be punished, that was what happened. He was very aware of how carefully his words must be chosen. The words we choose today might not affect the immediate fate of our lives, but they can cause our lives to be radically altered.

❹ According to Solomon, ours words hold the key to what? What does it mean?

Words can drastically affect our lives. ❺ <u>Recklessly spoken words can often hurt us deeply.</u> In Proverbs 12:18, Solomon compared reckless words to a sword. Have you ever spoken words without thinking about what their outcome would be? Have

❺ What results from reckless words?

you ever been the recipient of reckless words and known the pain they inflict? Foolish and sinful talk can start a path toward death. People have been killed over words. Proverbs 18:21 can be literally true; words can decide survival or death.

6 What are some results of foolish words?

7 What are some positive outcomes of wise words?

Words also affect our lives drastically in ways other than survival. **6** Foolish words can lead to rejection, loss of a career, the ruin of a marriage, the end of a friendship, or the beginning of a feud. **7** On the other hand, the fruits of wise words can be a friendship gained, a marriage established, a career secured, or a relationship restored. Basically, those who guard their mouths stay out of trouble (Prov. 21:23).

Destructive Words

Our words can be destructive. Making fun of the new kid at school because he dresses differently or making comments about someone else's hairstyle can cause serious damage. A teammate that criticizes another's efforts, a leader that heaps negativity on the group, or an overtly negative friend are using words destructively.

Solomon calls these types of comments rash words (Prov. 12:18). These words sometimes come from anger or from a bored and careless sense of humor. However, **8** they never come from a mind that is set on the Holy Spirit and filled with God's love for other people.

8 Where will destructive words never come from?

Solomon compares the effect of such words to a sword. Literal death may result from harsh words over a long period of time. Depression, resentment, or escalating retaliation may result. Public humiliation affects people far more than they usually let on. Students just like you tend to try to keep their lives in a false sense of "everything is OK" rather than show their disappointment. Guys are taught to "toughen up" as they grow older, and girls are criticized for being too emotional when they show how they are affected by words.

There is an alternative to stabbing someone with words. Words can be used to heal. **9** This involves refusing to use words to hurt and instead using words to encourage and uplift. Just as doctors become skillful with their hands, so Jesus' followers should become experts at encouraging. We need to learn to give positive feedback, express care and affection, and compliment with sincerity.

9 How can words be used to heal?

Speaking versus Listening

One of the greatest mistakes we can make is to speak without listening or without knowledge. This is sometimes referred to as "speaking out of turn." Wise people really do talk less than fools. A wise person is busy storing up knowledge (Prov. 10:14). A fool is busy revealing ignorance. **10** Fools don't understand listening because they are conceited and desire to show off (Prov. 18:2). They treasure the wrong things because

10 What characteristics cause foolish people to speak before listening?

of selfish motives. They generally think too highly of their ability to understand others. These foolish characteristics lead people to speak before listening (Prov. 18:13). Ten seconds of listening and a few seconds of thinking make a tongue's reply much wiser. When you listen, people know you care.

The Friend-Separator

Perhaps the habit of the tongue that generates the most anger is gossip. Proverbs 18:8 describes gossip as choice food that satisfies. Gossip is a strong temptation, and with some people it is treated like a delicacy. "You won't believe what I heard today!"

⓫ What could be an example of gossip?

⓫ Gossip is a verbal attack on someone without that person's knowledge. It may be relating something sinful or foolish someone else has done. It may involve bringing up painful stories from someone's past. It may simply be poking fun at someone behind his back. There are some legitimate occasions for relating damaging information about people to others. However, these reasons do not negate the prevalence of sinful gossip where the motivation is to take joy in another's folly and pain. In our sinful state, such cruelty can be a joy when we are greedy to increase our reputation by harming the reputation of others.

The consequences of gossip are horrendous. Proverbs 16:28 speaks of gossip separating close friends. Imagine a friend overhearing you tearing him apart to someone else, exposing a secret, or revealing something embarrassing. The hurtful power of gossip is real.

The Flattering Salesman

⓬ What is flattery?

⓬ Flattery is associated with people who want something and give insincere complements to get it. Sometimes flattery is more than simply one insincere compliment; instead, flattery can be a whole campaign designed to get someone on your side. Proverbs 29:5 states that flattery is like a net or a trap. Insincerity is lying, and lies are often discovered. People want to believe false compliments, but they are crushed when the real opinion is discovered.

The Tongue of the Wise

Words really do have power. A righteous man uses words to help others, to lift them up sincerely, and to promote humility. Protecting the reputation of others, giving out helpful knowledge, encouraging those who need it, speaking with modesty, and being truthful and kind with our words will bear fruit. People may be attracted to foul talk and gossip. However, when life gets serious, they'd much rather have a friend they can trust and whose words are wise. Besides, God rewards those who follow His wise way with their words.

SMALL-GROUP TIME:
Use this time to help students begin to integrate the truth they've learned into their lives while they connect with the other students in the group, the leaders, and with God.

After presenting the teaching material, ask students to divide back into small groups and discuss the "Do What?" questions. Small group facilitators should lead the discussions and set the tone by being open and honest in responding to each question.

 # Do What? *(15 MINUTES)*

Making It Personal

1. As you look back on the past week, give one area of your life in which your words got you in trouble?

2. According to James 3:3-8, the tongue is like a small fire that quickly devours an entire forest. How would you describe the words you use with your friends?

3. Who is one person who needs to hear some encouragement from you this week? How can you encourage that person?

4. Have you ever been the victim of gossip? What did that experience teach you?

5. Complete this sentence with the ending that most appropriately describes how you feel: "For me to change the way I use my words, I'm going to have to . . ."
   - ☐ hear God speak to me in an audible voice.
   - ☐ know that others will change their words too.
   - ☐ find a new group of friends that understands the negative effect words can have.
   - ☐ talk to God and get Him to help me.
   - ☐ have a close friend keep me accountable for my words.
   - ☐ take a vow of silence!
   - ☐ Other: _____

LifePoint Review

Small-group facilitators should reinforce the LifePoint for this session. Make sure that student's questions are invited and addressed honestly.

The words we say have a lasting impact. When we speak without thinking or gossip about others, we are hurting—not helping—others.

"Do" Points:

These "Do" Points will help you begin to experience this week's LifePoint. Be open and honest as you answer the questions within your small group.

1. <u>Commit to pay attention to your words.</u> When you speak without thinking about the words you use, you get careless. Take the time this week to think about the words you use. Think before you respond to people. Even if someone sounds like they are crazy, you don't have to be the one to point it out. Just because others laugh doesn't mean it's OK.
Do you struggle with speaking before you think?

2. <u>Notice people who need encouragement.</u> When you see someone who needs encouragement, take the time to talk to him or her with sincere words. Listen to him or her and respond with honest words.
How have you been affected by someone who encouraged you?

3. <u>Be on the lookout for flattery and gossip.</u> Many times when people get caught up in the excitement of conversation, they share things they shouldn't. Commit to look for flattery and gossip and LOVINGLY (not angrily or rudely) remind people that flattery and gossip can destroy friendships and people.
How often do you think you hear flattery and gossip used? In what situations do you think flattery and gossip are most often used?

Prayer Connection:

Be sure to end your session by asking students to share prayer needs with one another, especially as they relate to issues brought up by today's session.

This is the time to encourage, support, and pray for each other in our journeys to trust God and seek out real and personal encounters with Him.

Share prayer needs with the group, especially those related to hearing from and responding to God. Your group facilitator will close your time in prayer.

Encourage students to list prayer needs for others in their books so they can pray for one another during the week. Assign a student coordinator in each small group to gather the group's requests and e-mail them to the group members.

Prayer Needs:

Encourage students to dig a little deeper by completing a "Now What?" assignment before the next time you meet. Remind students about the "Get Ready" short daily Bible readings and related questions at the beginning of session 3.

 now What?

Deepen your understanding of who God is, and continue the journey you've begun today by choosing one of the following assignments to complete this week:

Option 1:
Go on a Flattery Safari. Be on the lookout for gossip or flattery. When you become aware of these moments, note them in a journal. Our discussion this week has suggested that we use our words to heal, build-up, or encourage. Respond to every opportunity for gossip or flattery by using words of encouragement. Be prepared to let everyone know how many times you were able to turn the table on destructive words during your safari.

Option 2:
Meditate on and memorize Proverbs 12:18. Meditating means repeating the verse over and over while you think about its meaning and ways you can apply it to your life. You can aid memorization by writing the verse on an index card and putting it where you can see it to practice. It is best to work on the verse daily for at least a week.

Bible Reference notes

Use these notes to deepen your understanding as you study the Bible on your own:

Proverbs 12:14   ***words of his mouth.*** That is, literally, the words he speaks (25:11). The good things we do and say bring rewards.

Proverbs 13:3   ***guards his mouth.*** Words produce consequences. James reinforced the wisdom of taming the tongue (Jas. 3:5-9).

Proverbs 18:2   A fool has no interest in learning, only in airing his own opinions.

Proverbs 18:8   ***choice food.*** This is an apt description of a "juicy" piece of gossip. Just as a delicacy is digested, gossip becomes a part of us and affects our attitudes.

Proverbs 18:21   ***Life and death.*** The tongue is the most powerful muscle in the body, but it also has incredible spiritual power in the lives of people. We can use use it to bring life or death to others and ourselves.

NOTES

Session

3

LIVING SMART WITH PARENTS

Connections Prep

MAIN LIFEPOINT: Learning to live life with godly wisdom makes family life easier. When we learn what our responsibility is in our family, life is better for everyone. God cares about your relationship with your family members.

BIBLE STUDY CHECKPOINTS: To reinforce the LifePoint, leaders and small-group facilitators should understand the following more detailed CheckPoints and "Do" Points.

LIFE CHANGE "DO" POINTS:
- Discover God's design for family
- Realize your responsibility as a family member
- Learn to respect parental wisdom

- Spend time searching God's Word for wisdom as it relates to family
- Find a time for your family to come together weekly to talk
- Meditate on and memorize one of the verses from this lesson

PREPARATION:
- ☐ Review the leader book for this session and prepare your teaching.
- ☐ Determine how you will subdivide students into small discussion groups.
- ☐ Recruit mature students or adults as small-group facilitators. Be sure these facilitators plan to attend.
- ☐ Use tape to create a maze on the floor of the meeting room for the "Say What?" activity

REQUIRED SUPPLIES:
- ☐ *Proverbs: Uncommon Sense* leader books for each group facilitator
- ☐ *Proverbs: Uncommon Sense* student books for each student
- ☐ Pens or pencils for each student
- ☐ Candy for the winners
- ☐ Tape for the maze
- ☐ Three blindfolds
- ☐ Furniture or other things that might be used for obstacles during "Say What?"

Get Ready

Read one of these short Bible passages each day and spend a few minutes wrapping your brain around it. Be sure to jot down any insights you discover.

MONDAY

Read Proverbs 17:6, 30:11-12, 17.
How important is your family to you? How do you treat your family?

TUESDAY

Read Proverbs 30:11-12, 17.
What is respect? How do you show respect to your family? Why do you think Solomon makes such strong statements about parents?

WEDNESDAY

Read Proverbs 1:8-9.
Why is listening to parents important? What are the rewards of listening to a parent's advice?

THURSDAY

Read Proverbs 4:1.
What kind of understanding have you gotten from your parents? Describe a time when your parents gave you instruction that really helped you.

FRIDAY

Read Proverbs 10:1, 15:20.

Do you have a responsibility to bring joy to your family? How can you bring joy to your family?

SATURDAY

Read Proverbs 23:24.

How does your family benefit when you gain wisdom?

3

SUNDAY

Read Luke 11:11-13.

What is the best gift you have ever received from a family member? What made that gift so special? How great is God's love and plan for your life as revealed in this passage?

LARGE-GROUP OPENING:
Get everyone's attention. Make announcements. Open your session with a prayer. Read the LifePoint to the students.

Ask about last week's "Now What?" exercises.

 LifePoint

Learning to live life with godly wisdom makes family life easier. When we learn what our responsibility is in our family, life is better for everyone. God cares about your relationship with your family members.

SMALL-GROUP TIME:
Instruct students to separate into smaller groups of 4-8, preferably in a circle configuration. Call on the mature student or adult leaders you recruited to facilitate each small group through this "Say What?" segment.

 # Say What? *(15 MINUTES)*

Random Question of the Week:

How is it that the villain always has kryptonite for Superman? Where do you get kryptonite, anyway? Is it special order?

Group Experience: A Walk in the Dark

Divide students into groups of three students. Instruct the groups to choose one person to be in the middle—the child. Direct them to choose another to get in front and lead the way—the parent. Instruct the remaining youth to be in back—a friend. To begin, the "child" from each group must put on a blindfold and navigate the maze . . . all at the same time! The first time through the maze, the blindfolded individuals may be escorted by the "parent" and the "friend." But after this initial turn, each "child" must go solo while avoiding the other blindfolded students and trying to remember the path through the maze.

Those who make it through get a prize! Those who don't must come back to the start, change roles, and give another player a turn. To make it more challenging, choose a different direction each turn.

After the exercise, ask these follow-up questions:

1. How important was it to have helpers on your journey? How does your family help you on your life journey?

2. What TV families seem to have it all together?

3. As you think about your family, how difficult is it to honestly evaluate your relationships with them?

 **So What?** *(30 MINUTES)*

LARGE-GROUP TIME:
Have the students turn to face the front for this teaching time. Be sure you can make eye contact with each student in the room. Encourage students to follow along and take notes in their student books.

Teaching Outline

I. The Importance of Family
A. Everyone experiences relational problems at some point and everyone responds differently
B. Families are very important to God
C. In not honoring our family ties, we fail to live the life God desires

II. Proverbs 17:6; 30:11-12,17; 1:8; 4:1; 10:1; 15:20; 23:24

3

III. God's Design
A. "Family" was at the beginning of God's plan
B. Today's families are under attack from the enemy
C. God created the family to train, equip, and encourage.
D. The family is the best environment for spiritual growth
E. Healthy families communicate
   1. They talk
   2. They listen
   3. They value one another

IV. A Big Responsibility
A. You are responsible for respecting your parents
   1. Respect through speech
   2. Respect through actions
   3. Respect through your response
B. You are responsible for learning from your parents
C. You are responsible for honoring your parents
D. You are not responsible for being in control of your home

Share the "So What?" teaching with your students. You may modify it to meet your needs.

V. Parental Wisdom
A. We gain wisdom by listening to our parents
B. Parents have already lived life from your place and perspective

Be sure to highlight the underlined information, which gives answers to the student book questions and fill-in-the-blanks (shown in the margins).

VI. Give Joy
A. Gather wisdom and show them what you have learned
B. Work hard

The Importance of Family

Everyone experiences difficult relationships. Some choose to simply let go of these relationships, while others decide to work on them with all of their might. Sometimes we work so hard on our relationships with our friends and classmates that we are too exhausted at the end of the day to spend time with our families.

We need to realize that families are very important to God. When we don't honor our families, we're not living the life that God desires for us to live. Even if you don't have perfect parents, you still have a responsibility to them. Today, let's learn how to make the best of the situations we have.

Learning from the Bible

**Before the session,
enlist a student to read
Proverbs 17:6;
30:11-12,17; 1:8; 4:1;
10:1; 15:20; 23:24.**

*Grandchildren are the crown of the elderly,
and the pride of sons is their fathers.—Proverbs 17:6*

*There is a generation that curses its father
and does not bless its mother.
There is a generation that is pure in its own eyes,
yet is not washed from its filth.—Proverbs 30:11-12*

*As for the eye that ridicules a father
and despises obedience to a mother,
may ravens of the valley pluck it out
and young vultures eat it.—Proverbs 30:17*

*Listen, my son, to your father's instruction,
and don't reject your mother's teaching.—Proverbs 1:8*

*Listen, my sons, to a father's discipline,
and pay attention so that you may gain understanding.—Proverbs 4:1*

*A wise son brings joy to his father,
but a foolish son, heartache to his mother.—Proverbs 10:1*

*A wise son brings joy to his father,
but a foolish one despises his mother.—Proverbs 15:20*

*The father of a righteous son will rejoice greatly,
and one who fathers a wise son will delight in him.—Proverbs 23:24*

LARGE-GROUP TIME CONTINUED:
This is the meat of the teaching time. Remind students to follow along and take notes in their student books.

As you share the "So What?" information with students, make it your own. Use your natural teaching style.

Emphasize underlined information, which gives answers to the student book questions or fill-in-the-blanks in the (shown in the margins).

❶ Who created the family? How was it created?

❷ What three purposes did God create the family for?

❸ What are traits of a healthy family?

❹ What is communication and why is it important to a family?

❺ What are three responsibilities you have as a family member?

❻ How can you show your parents respect?

God's Design

❶ Family was God's design at the very beginning. During the creation of the world, God made a man and then a woman to be man's companion. He told them that men and women would join together and become one flesh. Today, families are under attack by a very clever enemy. This enemy, Satan, seeks to use whatever is available to him to disrupt the institution God put together. One of the lies he uses suggests that students don't need parents. This, of course, is not biblical.

The words used to describe family today are not the words God would choose to use. You may hear friends talk about their dysfunctional families or discuss how crazy their parents are. Friends may talk about how they can't wait to get out of the house or how many problems their family has caused. This is not God's design for the family. **❷** God designed the family to train, equip, and encourage each other in order to live life with the skill we know as wisdom as they journey together. How can you gain wisdom in family matters without being a member of a family? It's impossible to do. A healthy family is the best environment for your spiritual growth. **❸** A healthy family has good communication among the family members and lives a life that grows in wisdom.

We think we know how to communicate because we talk to people every day. However, there is more to communication than talking. Last week we learned about the importance of our words and the impact they can have on others. Communicating is more than simply speaking words. **❹** Communication involves both talking and listening. If family members aren't talking and listening to each other, they can lose their feeling of value. We all want to be valued, and we can help others value us by valuing them and their ideas.

A Big Responsibility

As a family member, you have some pretty large responsibilities. **❺** You are responsible to respect your parents, learn from them, and bring them joy. Even when your parents make mistakes (Yes, parents do make mistakes!), you have a responsibility to love and honor them. Like Proverbs 17:6 states, you are to be proud of your parents, even when they dress weird and aren't the coolest people on earth.

Show Respect

❻ You can show respect to your parents in your speech, actions, and responses to their requests. We live in a culture that promotes parents as bumbling idiots. (Homer Simpson is just one example.) With such open slander against the family, why do you think it is so difficult today for a family to live a Godly life?

As you talk to your parents, you have the opportunity to listen and learn, and as your respect for your parents grows, the way you talk to them will change. You would probably never back-talk God, but you may back-talk your parents. You would consider it a horrible offense to tell God how stupid one of His commands is, yet you may fight with your parents because you think you are right. Many times, the way we respond to our parents comes from our desire to be in control. This is completely against what God has called us to do. We are called to respect our parents in Proverbs 30:11-12. When we are disrespectful to our parents, we are guilty of being filthy with sin (v. 12). As you desire to obey God by respecting your parents, you'll notice simple changes in the way you view them. When you see your parents' as an earthly representative of God, you have to realize they aren't perfect. They are trying to serve a perfect God, just like you are.

❻ Learning to control your rolling eyes, shrugging shoulders, and "smart" comments is a sign of respect for your parents. As you learn to respect your parents and their words, you will become more attentive to their requests. When they ask you to help by cleaning out the closet, the litter box, or taking out the trash, you understand it is an opportunity to serve God by respecting your parents.

A word of caution needs to be shared here. While the goal is to get you to love your parents and have a great family relationship with them, sometimes people can't relate. Some parents act in ways that are puzzling. If your parents are encouraging you to act in a way that is illegal or dangerous to your health or safety, you need to talk to a trusted adult. Talk to an adult that you trust in private and share what is going on with them. God's will is never for you to be abused (physically, emotionally, or sexually).

Parental Wisdom

❼ Give one reason you should obey your parents.

According to Proverbs 1:8 and 4:1, we should listen to the instruction of our parents so that we will gain understanding. ❼ We gain wisdom—the skill for living life— by listening to our parents and putting their words into our hearts. Parents typically aren't the horrible monsters we often portray them to be. ❼ They give you a curfew because they know the trouble that can arise without one. ❼ They encourage you to wear a jacket because they have been sick before. You can learn from your parents' wisdom. ❼ Your parents have had the opportunity to live life from your viewpoint and have learned from their mistakes. It may be hard to imagine, but your parents were once your age. As they grew older, their wisdom and skill for living increased. You too will mature and gather more wisdom as you grow older. It may be hard to believe in today's generation of Toys R Us kids who never want to grow up, but one day you will have the opportunity to move out of your parents' house, pay your own bills, and raise your own family. Some of you will choose to accept the challenge, and others will choose to rebel against the opportunity to gather wisdom.

The late Dr. Adrian Rogers shares this story about learning from his parents (paraphrase).

> *Imagine you are planning on driving on a cross-country trip and your parents are making the exact same trip as you are. Your parents chose to leave town 48 hours before you do so they have some distance between themselves and you and have the advantage of giving you tips on the road conditions from their own experience.*
>
> *On the third day, you receive a phone call from your father. He instructs you that you need to avoid a particular town because of severe road construction. He says he spent six hours in stand-still traffic by choosing to go the route he went, and he encourages you to take a simple detour that will definitely save you hours of waiting in traffic.*

Isn't that what parents do? Parents give you advice and direction to help you avoid the pitfalls and roadblocks of life. Knowing your parents were once your age and once struggled much like you do can help you see them from a different perspective. ❽ You can learn from your parents by listening to their instruction and heeding their advice when you know that it comes from the wisdom of having lived life at your age. Your parents may share stories of their own problems and struggles with you in order to keep you from making the same mistakes they did.

❽ **How can you learn from your parents' advice?**

Give Joy
You didn't have to do anything on the day you were born to make your parents smile. They smiled just because you were born. Whether your birth was picture-perfect or took 48 hours, your simple presence was a joy to your parents. As you grew up though, you probably started to do some things that frustrated them. As a child your rebellion was simple and easy to stop, but as you get older, your rebellion grows.

❾ **How can you bring joy to your parents?**

You can bring joy to your parents in a couple of ways. ❾ First, you can bring them joy by gathering wisdom. Show your parents that you are a learner. According to Proverbs 10:1 and 15:20, you bring joy to your family when you increase your wisdom. How can you show your wisdom to your family? Show your parents that you've learned from your mistakes and won't repeat them again. That will bring joy to your family. Your parents will notice the changes in you. ❾ You can also bring joy to your parents by working hard. Parents receive joy from your hard work because it encourages them in their parenting skills. Parents view you as an extension of them, so they receive joy when you work hard and are rewarded for a good job.

You have the ability to affect the emotional temperature of your home with your behavior. What you do has a direct relation to how your parents act toward you. If you decide to whole-heartedly pursue God and Godly wisdom in the area of your family, you can positively affect your household.

 # Do What? *(15 MINUTES)*

The Road Ahead

SMALL-GROUP TIME:
Use this time to help students begin to integrate the truth they've learned into their lives while they connect with the other students in the group, the leaders, and with God.

After presenting the teaching material, ask students to divide back into small groups and discuss the "Do What?" questions. Small-group facilitators should lead the discussions and set the tone by being open and honest in responding to each question.

1. What is the hardest thing for you to overcome in your relationship with your parents?

2. How difficult is it for you to imagine your parents were once your age? How does it feel to imagine that your parents once walked in your shoes?

3. How would you describe the perfect parent? Check all that apply.
   ☐ Gentle
   ☐ High expectations
   ☐ Driven
   ☐ Easy going
   ☐ Loving
   ☐ Helpful
   ☐ Demanding
   ☐ Easily won

4. Complete this sentence: "In order for my relationship to get better with my parents, I have to . . ."

LifePoint Review

Learning to live life with godly wisdom makes family life easier. When we learn what our responsibility is in our family, life is better for everyone. God cares about your relationship with your family members.

"Do" Points:

These "Do" Points will help you grab hold of this week's LifePoint. Be with yourself and others as you answer the questions within your small group.

1. Spend time searching God's Word for wisdom as it relates to family. Take the time to read more from Scripture about God's plan for the family.
   What can you learn from the Bible that will aid you in your family relationships?

2. Find a time for your family to come together weekly to talk. Talk about your day at school and ask your parents about their days. Listen when they talk. Talk about things that made you laugh, things that made you sad, and things that angered you. Learn to communicate with each other.
   When was the last time you spent time communicating with other members of your family?

3. Meditate on and memorize one of the verses from this lesson. Meditating means repeating the verse over and over while you think about its meaning and ways to apply it to your life. You can aid in scripture memorization by writing the verse on an index card and putting it where you can see it. It is best to work on the verse daily for at least a week.
   Which verse do you want to memorize this week?

Prayer Connection:

This is the time to encourage, support, and pray for each other in our journeys to trust God and seek out real and personal encounters with Him.

Share prayer requests you have with the group and make a note of any that others share. Your group facilitator will close your time in prayer.

Prayer Needs:

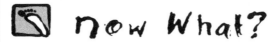 # now What?

Deepen your understanding of who God is and continue the journey you've begun today by choosing one of the following assignments to complete this week:

Option 1:

Take the time this week to meditate on the word "family". Read Ephesians 6:1-4. Look at your responsibility to your parents in this passage. Ask yourself the following questions:

- What is my role as a son or daughter?
- How well do I obey my parents?
- How important is my family to me?

Write a paragraph explaining what you have learned about family and your role in it. Be prepared to share your paragraph next week.

Option 2:

Plan a family meal at your house. You can simply have your family show up at an appointed time, or you can have them join you as you prepare a meal. The quality of the food isn't what is important here, what you do with the time you have together is. Discuss as a family your favorite memories together. Share what you have learned from this Bible study about your role in the family. After the meal, give each of your family members a note that tells them how much they mean to you.

Encourage students to dig a little deeper by completing a "Now What?" assignment before the next time you meet. Remind students about the "Get Ready" short daily Bible readings and related questions at the beginning of session 4.

Remind them that they are loved!

Bible Reference notes

Use these notes to deepen your understanding as you study the Bible on your own:

Proverbs 14:1

builds her house. The focus here is on "house," which refers to a home. Providing a solid foundation for her family is one of a wise woman's great achievements.

Proverbs 18:22

finds a good thing. A good wife is a treasure and gift from God. We need to appreciate the wife or husband that God has put into our life.

Proverbs 19:26

assaults. In this culture the care of elderly parents was the responsibility of sons and daughters.

Proverbs 23:16

innermost being. This literally means "kidneys" and refers to who we really are at the core of our being; the real, deepest person that we are.

Proverbs 27:8

man wandering. When a man leaves home, he leaves not only responsibility but also protection behind.

Session

4

BE COOL

Connections Prep

MAIN LIFEPOINT:
As we begin to understand the destructive effects of anger, we must learn practical ways to reduce conflict and control our tempers. The skill of living life with patience helps control anger.

To reinforce the LifePoint, leaders and small-group facilitators should understand the following more detailed CheckPoints and "Do" Points.

BIBLE STUDY CHECKPOINTS:
- Discover how to get control of anger
- Examine the different types of anger
- Learn to conceal offenses with love

LIFE CHANGE "DO" POINTS:
- Decide to give God your anger
- Commit to learn to diffuse anger in your relationships

PREPARATION:
☐ Review the leader book for this session and prepare your teaching.
☐ Determine how you will subdivide students into small discussion groups.
☐ Recruit mature students or adults as small-group facilitators. Be sure these facilitators plan to attend.

REQUIRED SUPPLIES:
☐ *Proverbs: Uncommon Sense* leader books for each group facilitator
☐ *Proverbs: Uncommon Sense* student books for each student
☐ Pens or pencils for each student

 **Get Ready**

Read one of these short Bible passages each day and spend a few minutes wrapping your brain around it. Be sure to jot down any insights you discover.

MONDAY

Read Proverbs 10:12 and 17:9.

How can love cover all things? What things do other people do that make you mad? How do you cover them with love?

TUESDAY

Read Proverbs 15:1.

What is your typical response when someone insults you? How did Jesus respond when people insulted Him?

WEDNESDAY

Read Proverbs 16:32.

What makes someone patient? Is patience considered honorable today? Why or why not? Who do you know that is a patient person?

THURSDAY

Read Proverbs 17:1.

Have you ever experienced a strife-filled home? If so, describe how you felt in that house.

FRIDAY　**Read Proverbs 17:14.**

What happens when a dam is breached? Have you ever been guilty of starting an argument that could have been avoided? How did you handle the situation? What was the outcome?

SATURDAY　**Read Proverbs 19:11.**

In what area of your life do you have the most patience? Is there anyone in your life that you have more patience with than others? Why does that person get more patience from you than others do?

SUNDAY　**Read James 1:19-20.**

Think about James' command to be slow to speak and quick to listen. What would happen if you consistently followed James' advice? How would your family life be different? How would your relationships with others be affected? What would be the negative results of acting this way?

LARGE-GROUP OPENING:
Get everyone's attention. Make announcements. Open your session with a prayer. Read the LifePoint to the students.

Ask about last week's "Now What?" exercises. Did anyone cook? Did anyone consider their roles as sons and daughters?

 LifePoint

As we begin to understand the destructive effects of anger, we must learn practical ways to reduce conflict and control our tempers. The skill of living life with patience helps control anger.

 # Say What? *(15 MINUTES)*

SMALL-GROUP TIME:
Instruct students to separate into smaller groups of 4-8, preferably in a circle configuration. Call on the mature student or adult leaders you recruited to facilitate each small group through this "Say What?" segment.

Random Question of the Week:
If vegetable oil is made from vegetables and corn oil is made from corn, what is canola oil made of?

Group Experience: Someone in My Hand

Play a game of "I Have Someone in My Hand." It's simple to play, difficult to catch on to, and frustrating to be the last one "in the know"!

Begin by saying, "I have someone in my hand. Who is it?" As students look around wondering what's going on, wait for someone to speak. If no one has responded with a guess after a couple of seconds, say, "It is me." Do it again except this time look directly at a particular student and again say, "I have someone in my hand. Who is it?"

The answer to the question is not the person in your hand, of course, nor is it the person you ask or look at. The answer to the question is the person who answers first. If the person on your left speaks first then that person is in your hand.

After a few rounds, some students will begin to understand what's going on. As they clue in, let them be the holder of someone else. Keep going until everyone understands how the game is played.

After the exercise, ask these follow-up questions:

1. How did it feel to try to figure out what was going on? Were you frustrated?

2. How did you feel once you found out how simple this game was?

3. How do people react when they get angry? Do they blow-up, pout, or sulk? Why?

4. Who is the most patient person you know? What makes that person so patient? How would you describe the way you feel about that person?

So What? *(30 MINUTES)*

LARGE-GROUP TIME:
Have the students turn to face the front for this teaching time. Be sure you can make eye contact with each student in the room. Encourage students to follow along and take notes in their student books.

Teaching Outline

I. The Anger Issue
  A. Anger is not a productive way to express your feelings
  B. Everybody has been angry at some point

II. Proverbs 10:12; 15:1; 16:32; 17:1,9,14; 19:11

III. Taking Control
  A. We can control anger
  B. We usually let our guard down around people we love
  C. Recognize the different kinds of anger

IV. Anger and Love
  A. Anger can lead to hate—the opposite of love
  B. Understand that "hate" can mean "not preferred."
    1. This suggests a choice
    2. To hate means that we have chosen ourselves over someone else
  C. Love, on the other hand, means "to prefer."

TEACHING FOR THE LARGE GROUP:
Share the "So What?" teaching with your students. You may modify it to meet your needs.

Be sure to highlight the underlined information, which gives answers to the student book questions and fill-in-the-blanks (shown in the margins).

V. Love Conceals Offenses
  A. We should take up for those that we love—even when offended
  B. Offenses don't have to be addressed right away
  C. The enemy works through our anger and compulsion to anger

VI. Patience
  A. Acquiring patience means "conquering" yourself
  B. We must be guarded about letting our patience wear thin around those with whom we're most familiar

VII. Anger in the Family

VIII. Stopping a Conflict

The Anger Issue

Anger is not a proper way to respond to our feelings. We cover our outbursts and fits of anger by saying things like, "I couldn't help it, I was just so angry," and we expect people to overlook faults in our lives. It is one thing to have a righteous anger over godly things like Jesus did in Matthew 21, but it's something completely different to get angry and have an explosion over someone getting our new shoes dirty, scratching our favorite CD, or changing our plans. Have you ever been angry? The probability is that you have. Let's look at some verses from Proverbs that relate to anger.

Learning from the Bible

Hatred stirs up conflicts,
but love covers all offenses.–Proverbs 10:12

A gentle answer turns away anger,
but a harsh word stirs up wrath.–Proverbs 15:1

Patience is better than power,
and controlling one's temper, than capturing a city.–Proverbs 16:32

Better a dry crust with peace
than a house full of feasting with strife.–Proverbs 17:1

Whoever conceals an offense promotes love,
but whoever gossips about it separates friends.–Proverbs 17:9

To start a conflict is to release a flood;
stop the dispute before it breaks out.–Proverbs 17:14

A person's insight gives him patience,
and his virtue is to overlook an offense.–Proverbs 19:11

Taking Control

We act like controlling our anger is impossible. We tell others that anger just gets the best of us and they don't understand how angry we get. The fact is that we can control our anger. There is strong evidence of this in the way we show anger toward some people and control anger around others. ❶ <u>When we want something from somebody or need to look good in someone's eyes, we overlook offenses and</u>

Before the session, enlist a student to read Proverbs 10:12; 15:1; 16:32; 17:1,9,14; 19:11.

LARGE-GROUP TIME CONTINUED: This is the meat of the teaching time. Remind students to follow along and take notes in their student books.

As you share the "So What?" information with students, make it your own. Use your natural teaching style.

Emphasize <u>underlined information</u>, which gives answers to the student book questions or fill-in-the-blanks in the (shown in the margins).

❶ **What evidence is there that we actually can control our anger?**

52

irritations. For example, if you are trying to get a date with that special someone, you tolerate irritations because you don't want to scare him or her off. Students also control their anger toward teachers in hopes of being rewarded with good grades. We find ways to control anger when it is clearly in our best interest to do so. When we let down our guard, we say we cannot control our anger. The sad thing is that this usually happens around those we love.

Types of Anger

❷ What are the different kinds of anger?

There are different kinds of anger and anger reactions. ❷ One familiar kind of anger is the short burst of temper. An out-of-control temper often opens the door to violence. Another kind of anger is the slow-seething resentment. A step worse is blatant hatred or loathing for someone else.

When a parent yells, "You always have to make things difficult!" you feel your anger rise and you yell back, "What's difficult is living with you!" Arguments, tension, annoyance, and resentment are all too common. Displays of temper can be embarrassing. Harsh words can destroy relationships. Constant complaining and annoying displays of disrespect can permanently damage marriages. Explosive tempers can do even worse; they can lead to violence. Anger is rarely justified. In Proverbs, Solomon reveals the attitudes behind anger and gives us the tools to control it.

Anger and Love

Anger can lead to hatred, which is the opposite of love. Solomon says that "love covers all offenses" but "hatred stirs up conflicts" (Prov. 10:12). It is important to understand the meaning of the word hate in the Bible. The languages of the Bible, Hebrew and Greek, sometimes have different shades of meaning for words that we are familiar with in English. In the Bible, hate does not necessarily mean emotional dislike. For example, Genesis 29:31 states that God saw that "Leah was unloved." The word for unloved here is hated, but Jacob did not hate Leah in the sense that he emotionally detested her. He simply did not prefer her; he preferred Rachel.

❸ How does love regard the other person?

Understanding the meaning of hatred is crucial to understanding Proverbs 10:12. Solomon does not mean that we start fights by emotionally detesting people. In fact, we often start fights with people we love! We don't mean to lash out at those we love, and we don't emotionally detest them. Rather, we start fights with people because we do not prefer them or their actions. Who do we choose in their place? Usually, we choose ourselves. ❸ Love, on the other hand, prefers the other person. Love does not want to cause a conflict unless there is a good reason. Love is not selfish (1 Cor. 13:5). Anger is almost always selfish and is very jealous.

Love Conceals Offenses

❹ According to Proverbs 10:12 and 17:9, what does love do with offenses?

❹ When people we love, offend us, our first move should be to cover the offense or conceal it (Prov. 10:12; 17:9). Rather than explode and let them receive what they have "coming to them," we should overlook it. However, there are times when an offense must be addressed. These times will vary from situation to situation. Most of the time we know when we're in one of these situations. The problem is, we often assume that any offense against us must be addressed—and right away. This just isn't the case. In almost every case the best response will include patience.

For example, a young man with an interest in a young woman will be forgiving and understanding when she is flustered about something. Her angry words or behavior may be wrong and harmful, but the heat of anger is not the time to correct her actions. She needs someone to listen. Also, parents who require time to wind down in the evenings after a day of work can also be shown love through understanding.

The opposite reaction, reacting to anger with anger, isn't an effective response. Rolling your eyes, glaring, huffing, and yelling are poor responses to small offenses. While these are natural teenage defenses and actions, they are not good reactions.

In fact, one of the greatest tools Solomon gives us to combat conflict is a kind word. A gentle answer in response to angry words or an insult is incredibly disarming (Prov. 15:1). A person who directs wrath against you expects you to come back at him with wrath. When someone says something incredibly rude or expresses anger toward you, try responding with genuine kindness. You'll be surprised at the reaction you receive.

❺ How does the enemy work through insults and anger?

The enemy of kind words, of course, is Satan. Given his villain status, he seems always ready to take advantage of an opportunity to get mad. ❺ If someone throws an insult our way, we think, *I've got to get him back so I don't look weak or stupid.* Satan cheers this sort of mentality. A better strategy is to attempt to disarm your anger with kindness. This response goes against everything the enemy whispers. When you respond to anger with kindness, you never look weak or stupid. You become the rational voice in the conversation. As a result, you may turn a bad situation into something good.

Patience, an Undesired Virtue

People often say they don't want to be patient because patience requires that they endure annoyance. In reality, patience is an admired quality. Solomon wrote that a patient person is better than a war hero (Prov. 16:32). ❻ He explains that a general who conquers a city fights a difficult but defeatable foe, but a person who is patient through annoying circumstances defeats a foe most people consider invincible.

Controlling your temper is just that: being in control of yourself. It is difficult, but you are capable of doing it. You already do it when the cost of losing your temper is too high. Most people are able to be patient around a superior or someone whose goodwill they need. We tend to let our guard down, though, in front of friends and family. We often take their love for granted because we know that these relationships will survive a little conflict. As a result, we take advantage of the people we say we love and bend over backward for the people who test us. Why? Because we are selfish; we are on the lookout for what we can get from a situation and relationship.

Anger in the Family

Because of our tendency to take the goodwill of our family for granted, we have more fights in the family than out of it. Consequently, we end up making our loved ones and ourselves unhappy with conflict (Prov. 17:1). Anger ruins many vacations and family outings. Even beaches and amusement parks lose their luster when quarrels prevail.

Solomon's wisdom on anger applies to the family very well. Overlook offenses (Prov. 19:11). Respond gently to anger and insulting language (Prov. 15:1). Prefer the other person over yourself (Prov. 10:12) and learn how to stop a conflict.

Stopping a Conflict

❼ Trouble can be stopped before it gets out of hand. Solomon compares conflict to water released through a dam (Prov. 17:14). The time to use a gentle word or overlook an offense is as early as possible. If you wait until a fight is well under way, the flood may be impossible to stop. In today's society, people want to win, not resolve. However, as followers of Jesus, we are called to be patient. Patience causes us to depend on what God is teaching us and rely on the wisdom we are learning from Him.

❻ How is a patient person a war hero?

❼ What is the best time to stop a fight?

4

SMALL-GROUP TIME:

Use this time to help students begin to integrate the truth they've learned into their lives while they connect with other students in the group, the leaders, and with God.

After presenting the teaching material, ask students to divide back into small groups and discuss the "Do What?" questions. Small group facilitators should lead the discussions and set they tone by being open and honest in responding to each question.

Small-group facilitators should reinforce the LifePoint for this session, make sure that student's questions are invited and addressed honestly.

 # Do What? *(15 MINUTES)*

1. What is the most embarrassing thing you have done when you were angry?

2. Why was it embarrassing?

2. Check which response is easier for you:
   - ☐ To walk away from a conflict
   - ☐ To dive-in with insults
   - ☐ To help resolve the problem
   - ☐ To remain quiet and uninvolved
   - ☐ Other:

LifePoint Review

As we begin to understand the destructive effects of anger, we must learn practical ways to reduce conflict and control our tempers. The skill of living life with patience helps control anger.

"Do" Points:

These "Do" Points will help you realize this week's LifePoint. It's okay to be open and honest about your doubts as you answer the questions within your small group.

1. <u>Decide to give God your anger.</u> The way to make a difference in your struggle with anger is to actually do something about it and give it to God.
   Are you seeking God in the areas of your life affected by your anger? Do you really want to let go of these areas of anger in your life?

2. <u>Commit to learn to diffuse anger in your relationships.</u> When you get angry with people, you can affect their lives by showing them how you avoid letting anger rule your life. You can help others learn the skill of living life with patience.
   What are two things you can do to diffuse the anger in your relationships?

Be sure to end your
session by asking
students to share prayer
needs with one another,
especially as they relate
to issues brought up by
today's session.

Encourage students to
list prayer needs for
others in their books
so they can pray for
one another during the
week. Assign a student
coordinator in each
small group to gather
the group's requests and
e-mail them to the
group members.

Prayer Connection:

This is the time to encourage, support, and pray for each other in our journeys to trust God and seek out real and personal encounters with Him.

Take time now to encourage and support each other by sharing your prayer concerns and writing down the requests of others in your group. Your facilitator will close your time in prayer.

Prayer Needs:

9

 now What?

Encourage students to dig a little deeper by completing a "Now What?" assignment before the next time you meet. Remind students about the "Get Ready" short daily Bible readings and related questions at the beginning of session 5.

Remind them again this week that they are loved!

Deepen your understanding of who God is and continue the journey you've begun today by choosing one of the following assignments to complete this week:

Option 1:
Make a list of the actions of others that cause you to be angry. When someone commits an offense that angers you, make a note of it. Take the time during the week to pray over your list. As you continue to pray over your list and add to it, be sure to make notes of times when you avoid anger and conflict.

Option 2:
If you are artistic, take time this week to create a drawing or painting of something in your life that causes you anger. Talk to God about your anger as you are creating your artwork. When you are finished with your artwork, write Proverbs 19:11 somewhere on it. You can write on the back of your art or on the front. Take the time to pray about your anger and be prepared next week to share your art with your group. If you feel comfortable, give your piece of art to someone in your small group as a symbol of releasing your anger over that issue. Have that person pray with you as you release this aspect of your anger.

Bible Reference notes

Use these notes to deepen your understanding as you study the Bible on your own:

Proverbs 15:1   Much like James, Proverbs makes the point that the way we use speech tells a lot about what kind of people we are (James 3:5-8). Whether we use gentle or harsh words, our conversation reflects our character.

Proverbs 17:1   *feasting.* This refers to feasting provided for by a family's peace offering. See Leviticus 7:12-17.

Proverbs 17:9   *conceals.* To conceal a sin is to literally overwhelm it with forgiveness and love.

NOTES

Session

5

PRIDE ROCK: THE HUMBLE SOLUTION

Connections Prep

MAIN LIFEPOINT:
Pride causes destruction in our lives. Pride is sneaky. It creeps into our lives and is often difficult to recognize. Humility is the best weapon we can use to combat pride in our lives.

To reinforce the LifePoint, leaders and small-group facilitators should understand the following more detailed CheckPoints and "Do" Points.

BIBLE STUDY CHECKPOINTS:
· Recognize the destructive nature of pride
· Discover the benefits of humility
· Learn how to be humble

LIFE CHANGE "DO" POINTS:
· Commit to spend time talking to God about others
· Discover areas of pride in your life
· Develop the ability to be real

PREPARATION:
☐ Review the leader book for this session and prepare your teaching.
☐ Determine how you will subdivide the students into small discussion groups.
☐ Recruit mature students or adults as small-group facilitators. Be sure these facilitators plan to attend.
☐ Cue *Beauty and the Beast* to chapter 8: "Gaston."

REQUIRED SUPPLIES:
☐ *Proverbs: Uncommon Sense* leader books for each group facilitator
☐ *Proverbs: Uncommon Sense* student books for each student
☐ Pens or pencils for each student
☐ A DVD or VHS cassette of *Beauty and the Beast*

 Get Ready

Read one of these short Bible passages each day and spend a few minutes wrapping your brain around it. Be sure to jot down any insights you discover.

MONDAY   **Read Proverbs 11:2; 16:18.**
Do you ever struggle with pride? When are you most likely to deal with it? What causes you to be proud?

TUESDAY   **Read Proverbs 18:12; 25:6-7.**
What does the word *humble* mean? How is a humble person treated today? What is special about a humble person?

WEDNESDAY   **Read Proverbs 27:1.**
How can boasting about the future make you guilty of pride? What is going to happen to you tomorrow? What will happen to you in the future?

THURSDAY   **Read Proverbs 27:2,21.**
Is it wrong to receive praise from others? How can you get others to give you praise? When do you give praise to others?

FRIDAY   **Read Proverbs 12:9; 16:19.**

Have you ever twisted the truth to make yourself look better to others? Explain. Why did you desire to make yourself look better?

SATURDAY   **Read Proverbs 22:4; James 4:6.**

When you talk to God, how do you approach Him? Do you think God owes you something? Why or why not? Why do you think God rewards humility?

SUNDAY   **Philippians 2:8.**

What is humbling about Jesus' experience? Why did Jesus become human? What is the motivation for Jesus' humility?

LARGE-GROUP OPENING:
Get everyone's attention. Make announcements. Open your session with a prayer. Read the LifePoint to the students.

Ask about last week's "Now What?"

 LifePoint

Pride causes destruction in our lives. Pride is sneaky. It creeps into our lives and is often difficult to recognize. Humility is the best weapon we can use to combat pride in our lives.

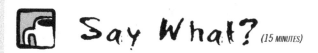 **Say What?** *(15 MINUTES)*

Random Question of the Week:
Why do we drive on a parkway and park on a driveway?

Group Experience: Who Is the Beast?

After watching the movie clip, ask students the following questions then discuss this extreme case of pride in small groups:

1. As the scene opens, Gaston appears to be in the dumps for some reason. What does it require to get him back in good spirits?

2. How would you describe Gaston?
   - ❑ He's my hero!
   - ❑ If I saw him coming my direction, I'd turn around and go the other way
   - ❑ I want to be like him: big, powerful, good-looking
   - ❑ He's a person I'd really like to be around: sensitive and caring
   - ❑ He's full of himself
   - ❑ He's the perfect man

3. When Gaston is in good spirits and having a good time, what does that mean for the rest of the group?

4. Is Gaston a person you'd enjoying being around? Why or why not?

5. In your opinion, what is Gaston's disgrace?

The point here, of course, is that Gaston is about as prideful as it gets. His only recreation is playing a rendition of "How Great Am I?" with his "friends." It's certainly no fun for his friends and it rings very hollow for Gaston himself. The word "friends" here is used very loosely since their only function in Gaston's life is to make him into more than he is . . . because he absolutely needs it.

This isn't to say that we shouldn't reach out to these types. Rather, the message this scene delivers suggests the dangers of self-absorbed pride that Proverbs preaches avoiding.

Sidebar:

Show the Beauty and the Beast segment mentioned in your preparation to the large group before breaking into smaller groups. The clip runs for approximately 3:30.

SMALL-GROUP TIME: Instruct students to separate into smaller groups of 4-8, preferably in a circle configuration. Call on the mature student or adult leaders you recruited to facilitate each small group through this "Say What?" segment.

#1 Everybody else has to tell him how great he is while they themselves come off looking silly. It's the only way to get his attention.

Note #3: It means that he's going to build himself up while tearing everyone else down.

LARGE-GROUP TIME:
Have the students turn to face the front for this teaching time. Be sure you can make eye contact with each student in the room. Encourage students to follow along and take notes in their student books.

 # So What? *(30 MINUTES)*

Teaching Outline

I. Who Is the Beast?
A. Excessive pride is far from beautiful
B. Pride just needs more and more fuel; it's a beast that demands to be fed

II. Pride—The Destroyer
A. Pride works to destroy relationships
B. Humility allows relationships ample room to grow

III. Proverbs 11:2; 12:9; 16:18-19; 18:12; 22:4; 25:6-7; 27:1-2,21

IV. Beware the Lion Cub
A. Pride is harmless—maybe even cute—at first
B. Pride can grow into an enormous beast
C. It's good to have rules for dealing with pride
D. Humility: the opposite of pride

V. The Way to Disgrace
A. Presumption is a quick road to pride
B. Falling from the tightrope of pride is painful
C. Pride is often followed by disgrace

VI. A Life God Rewards
A. An "others first" attitude is spiritual
B. Humility recognizes God for who He is

TEACHING FOR THE LARGE GROUP:
Share the "So What?" teaching with your students. You may modify it to meet your needs.

Be sure to highlight the underlined information, which gives answers to the student book questions and fill-in-the-blanks (shown in the margins).

Pride—The Destroyer

Pride destroys relationships while humility allows relationships to grow. When pride enters into a relationship, it affects everyone involved. Whether you think you are better than someone or feel that someone thinks they are better than you, pride's effects are damaging. No one likes to be around someone who struggles with pride. Pride causes even the closest friends to part.

From 2000 until 2002, the Los Angeles Lakers were the NBA's World Champion. They held the title each of those three years. They seemed to have it all: the best players and the best coach. They seemed to be unstoppable, yet their pride both on the court and off became inescapable. Players began to complain about playing time because they thought they were the best. Teammates began to bicker. It didn't take long for players and the coach to depart the once great Lakers team. In the 2004-2005 season, the Lakers failed to even qualify for the playoffs. This was one of only four times they hadn't qualified since 1960! Pride was definitely to blame. Let's look at some Scriptures that discuss the areas of pride and humility.

Learning from the Bible

Before the session, enlist a student to read Proverbs 11:2; 12:9; 16:18-19; 18:12; 22:4; 25:6-7; 27:1-2,21.

When pride comes, disgrace follows,
but with humility comes wisdom.—Proverbs 11:2

Better to be dishonored, yet have a servant,
than to act important but have no food.—Proverbs 12:9

Pride comes before destruction,
and an arrogant spirit before a fall.
Better to be lowly of spirit with the humble
than to divide plunder with the proud.—Proverbs 16:18-19

Before his downfall a man's heart is proud,
but before honor comes humility.—Proverbs 18:12

The result of humility is fear of the LORD,
along with wealth, honor, and life.—Proverbs 22:4

Don't brag about yourself before the king,
and don't stand in the place of the great;
for it is better for him to say to you, "Come up here!"
than to demote you in plain view of a noble.—Proverbs 25:6-7

Don't boast about tomorrow,
for you don't know what a day might bring.
Let another praise you, and not your own mouth—
a stranger, and not your own lips.—Proverbs 27:1-2

Silver is tested in a crucible, gold in a smelter,
and a man, by the praise he receives.—Proverbs 27:21

LARGE-GROUP TIME
CONTINUED:
This is the meat of the
teaching time. Remind
students to follow along
and take notes in their
student books.

As you share the
"So What?" information
with students, make
it your own. Use your
natural teaching style.

Emphasize underlined
information, which
answers the student
book questions or fill-in-
the-blanks (shown in the
margins).

❶ What is real
humility?

❷ What are some
examples of false
humility?

❸ What are the
benefits of humility for
us? For others?

Beware the Lion Cub

Pride is not something that we can walk away from easily. Pride creeps into our lives a little bit at a time. It starts out as something that seems harmless—like a lion cub. Who hasn't looked at a baby lion cub and thought, "How cute! I would LOVE to have one of those as a pet"? Most of us have, but probably none of us has ever actually received a pet lion cub. Why aren't lion cubs popular pets? It's because lion cubs grow up to be adult lions, and adult lions are dangerous. Regardless of how great your animal training skills are, having a lion roam around your house or your neighborhood is dangerous. We know the dangers associated with having a lion, so we develop little rules like, "No pets allowed that can eat you!" to keep us alive. It's important for us to create rules that are also associated with pride.

We all share the problem of pride to some extent. Whether it's dealing with being the best athlete in school, the best member of the band, the smartest kid in class, the best artist, or simply thinking we are one of these, we struggle with pride. We despise pride when we see it in others and make sure to avoid situations where the pride of others can affect us, but we let our own pride run wild in our lives.

The opposite of pride is humility. ❶ Real humility is putting others before you and regarding yourself as less important than others. Many people, however, live with a false view of humility. ❷ Some people view humility as a need to feel negative and say things that are degrading about themselves like, "I'm probably going to be horrible at this, but I guess I'll give it a try." That's not humility at all. Others, like students who know they have great musical talent and deny it because they want people to tell them how great they are, have fake modesty.

A perfect picture of humility is Jesus coming as a helpless infant and dying for our sins. The Apostle Paul discusses the humility he would like to see the followers of Jesus adopt. In Philippians 2:5, Paul describes we should have the same attitude of the mind that Jesus had. Jesus was humble. His humility is illustrated by the way he lowered Himself to help others. Paul doesn't mean Jesus lowered Himself in a snobbish way but in a authentically loving way. He did not consider His importance greater than the need of people like you and me.

❸ Humility is an attitude that is good for us and for others because it frees us from deceit and ego. It also reduces depression because we spend more time thinking of others and less time thinking of ourselves. Humility is good for others because it causes us to support and help the people God places in our lives. Most importantly, humility is a fact of life here on earth. No one is more important than Jesus Christ. If Jesus had refused to lower Himself and save us, we would not celebrate His love. We, who are far less important than He is, should follow His example and believe that our loved ones, friends, and neighbors are more important than we are.

4 What are some other words for pride?

4 <u>Pride can be described as presumption, selfishness, arrogance, conceit, smugness, and vanity.</u> All the traits that we despise in others and struggle with ourselves are wrapped up in pride.

A perfect illustration of humility's effect on us is the underdog syndrome. Whether it's in sports or school, we tend to root for the underdog. We like to hear "rags to riches" stories of singers who were waiting tables last year to pay the rent and this year have number one singles. We love to hear "victory against the odds" stories about guys like Kurt Warner, the former quarterback of the St. Louis Rams, who led his team to victory in the Super Bowl. Kurt was bagging groceries at an Iowa grocery store the year before. Why do we love humility so much even though it is one of the hardest traits to possess? **5** <u>The answer would have to be that God filled us with a love for humility. No one exhibits humility quite like God who, being the highest, made Himself low for our sake.</u>

5 Why do we love humility so much?

The Way to Disgrace

A common word for pride in the Bible is presumption. Solomon paints a perfect picture of presumption and its results. He describes a man who boasts in the presence of the king and assumes a place of importance in the king's hall. However, the man's plan to increase his importance fails when the king publicly chastises him (Prov. 25:6-7). **6** <u>When we are presumptuous, we assume a higher place than we should.</u> We think we're the best player on the team, guaranteed to start and be the Most Valuable Player, only to find ourselves sitting on the bench during the state championship or (worse yet) cut from the team to make room for a better player!

6 What is presumption?

Pride leads to a fall. If you walk on a high path, you will most likely fall and get hurt. However, the one who walks on a low road has less distance to fall. Think about it this way, would you rather walk on a 2x4 between two buildings 100 feet in the air without a net or safety device, or on a 2x4 that is on the sidewalk? Some daredevils would jump at the chance to walk 100 feet off the ground just to be able to show people they can do it. Sound like pride? Would they do it if no one was watching? Some people would say yes for the pure adrenaline rush and the chance to tell everyone else what they had done, while others would only do it if someone was there to watch them and be amazed.

Walking on a 2x4 on the sidewalk is different though. Who wants to do something like that? Everyone can do that right? When we are humble, we are free from the need to perform for the praise of others. Instead, we exist for the acceptance of God and God alone.

❼ Why does pride lead to a downfall?

❼ There are three reasons why pride is often followed by disgrace. First, the proud person sets himself up to fall by assuming a place from which the only way out is down. Second, people tend to resent (and want to bring down) a proud person. Third, God resists the proud and allows them to be their own downfall (Jas. 4:6). You undoubtedly know someone who has thought they were "all that" only to be disgraced by their failure to perform. Pride demands a lifetime of performance. When the excitement is gone, so is the crowd, and the prideful person plummets like a skydiver without a parachute.

A Life God Rewards

A "me-first" attitude is natural, but an "others-first" attitude is spiritual. Humility is not as hard to obtain as people think. It is not deciding that you are no good at anything; in fact, it is not about you at all. Humility is the habit and attitude of thinking about others more than yourself. Humility is simply learning to delight in others.

God is humble. It seems strange to say that since God is the perfect, all-powerful, most important person in the universe. Yet, it is true. God delights in others, even though He alone has the right to think only of Himself.

And a person who is humble is a person whom God honors (Prov. 22:4). A truly humble person will not only realize others are more important, but they will also realize that God is of the highest importance. As a result, a humble person becomes complete by fearing God. God rewards humility. The rewards may not be in the areas of financial success or fame but in the joy of grace, love, and peace.

SMALL-GROUP TIME:
Use this time to help students begin to integrate the truth they've learned into their lives while they connect with the other students in the group, the leaders, and with God.

After presenting the teaching material, ask students to divide back into small groups and discuss the "Do What?" questions. Small-group facilitators should lead the discussions and set the tone by being open and honest in responding to each question.

 # Do What? *(15 MINUTES)*

1. How has pride affected you personally? How has it damaged your relationships?

2. How do you feel when someone is prideful? Do you enjoy being around them?

3. How is pride a part of your life? Check all that apply.
   - ☐ I don't struggle with pride; ask anyone, they'll tell you how humble I am.
   - ☐ I tend to focus on what I deserve in relationships and situations.
   - ☐ I have a hard time focusing on others. I'm more worried about "ME".
   - ☐ I try hard to focus on others, but pride keeps creeping back in my life when I'm not looking.
   - ☐ Other:

Small-group facilitators should reinforce the LifePoint for this session. Make sure that student's questions are invited and addressed honestly.

LifePoint Review

Pride causes destruction in our lives. Pride is sneaky. It creeps into our lives and is often difficult to recognize. Humility is the best weapon we can use to combat pride in our lives.

"Do" Points:

These "Do" Points will give you a handle on week's LifePoint. Be open and honest as you answer the questions within your small group.

1. <u>Commit to spend time talking to God about others.</u> The best way to combat pride is with humility. Humility comes from thinking about others more than yourself and seeing others as worth your effort.
   How much time do you spend talking to God about others?

2. <u>Search for areas of pride in your life.</u> Pride comes in many shapes and sizes. It can creep in quietly when you aren't alert.
   What do you need to do in your life to be on the lookout for pride?

3. <u>Develop the ability to be real.</u> Focusing on the approval of others takes your focus off of God and keeps you from being concerned about others. When you are fake, people don't get the chance to know the real you.
   How have you tried to "cover over" your faults, mistakes, and the real you?

Be sure to end your session by asking students to share prayer needs with one another, especially as they relate to issues brought up by today's session.

Encourage students to list prayer needs for others in their books so they can pray for one another during the week. Assign a student coordinator in each small group to gather the group's requests and e-mail them to the group members.

Prayer Connection:

This is the time to encourage, support, and pray for each other in our journeys to discover who Jesus really is and how much He cares for each of us. Share prayer needs with the group, especially those related to knowing and connecting with Jesus. Your group facilitator will close your time in prayer.

Prayer Needs:

Encourage students to dig a little deeper by completing a "Now What?" assignment before the next time you meet. Remind students about the "Get Ready" short daily Bible readings and related questions at the beginning of session 6.

 # now What?

Deepen your understanding of who God is and continue the journey you've begun today by choosing one of the following assignments to complete this week:

Option 1:
Focus on others this week. Don't make a show of what you're doing. Spend time praying for people when they don't know it. Look for opportunities to help. Pick up a pencil that someone drops in the hallway. Hold the door for your friends as you go into class. Be creative. Find ways to take the focus off of getting what you deserve this week; instead, give your attention to the needs of others.

Option 2:
Make a list this week of times in your life when you sense pride. Each day, find a quiet time and review your list. Pray about the pride that you discover and thank God for helping you recognize the arrogance that's in your life. Look over the verses from Proverbs from this lesson and allow God to change you. Be prepared to share your list with your small group next week.

Bible Reference notes

Use these notes to deepen your understanding as you study the Bible on your own:

Proverbs 11:2 — *humility.* This refers to putting both God and others before yourself. See also Micah 6:8.

Proverbs 12:9 — *have a servant.* It's better to be of humble circumstances working for yourself than acting big yet having nothing to eat.

Proverbs 25:6 — *place of the great.* We should never "toot our own horn" or honor ourselves. The circumstance here is a feast, in which we are instructed never to take the place of honor, assuming our own greatness.

Proverbs 27:21 — *crucible.* Our response to praise is a test of our true character. Silver and gold are purified with heat. Our character is also tested in the heat of life.

Session

6

THE BEST
4-LETTER WORD

Connections Prep

MAIN LIFEPOINT: A kind and loving spirit is characteristic of a Christian's life. People see Christ in you through the love and kindness you show others.

To reinforce the LifePoint, leaders and small-group facilitators should understand the following more detailed CheckPoints and "Do" Points.

BIBLE STUDY CHECKPOINTS:
- Understand the importance of kindness
- Recognize a kind and loving spirit as part of a Christ-like life
- Learn to treat people with kindness

LIFE CHANGE "DO" POINTS:
- Learn to recognize "me-centered" thinking
- Choose to become a loyal person
- Develop ways to show kindness to others

PREPARATION:
- ☐ Review the leader book for this session and prepare your teaching.
- ☐ Determine how you will subdivide students into small discussion groups.
- ☐ Recruit mature students or adults as small-group facilitators. Be sure these facilitators plan to attend.

REQUIRED SUPPLIES:
- ☐ *Proverbs: Uncommon Sense* leader books for each group facilitator
- ☐ *Proverbs: Uncommon Sense* student books for each student
- ☐ Pens or pencils for each student
- ☐ Fifteen round stickers for each student (you can find them in most large discount stores—or you can make them yourself with construction paper and masking tape)
- ☐ Candy as a prize for the "Pay It Forward" winner

This "Get Ready" section is primarily for the students, but leaders and facilitators will benefit from these devotionals as well.

 Get Ready

Read one of these short Bible passages each day and spend a few minutes wrapping your brain around it. Be sure to jot down any insights you discover.

MONDAY

Read Proverbs 14:21; 21:21.
How are kindness and happiness linked? Why would a kind person be honored? Who do you show kindness to—friends, strangers, or both?

TUESDAY

Read Proverbs 12:25.
How have you benefited from a kind word? How do you encourage people with kind words? When was the last time you used a kind word to encourage someone else?

WEDNESDAY

Read Proverbs 20:6.
Has a friend ever promised to do something for you and failed to do it? How did that make you feel? Have you ever failed to follow up on a promise to a friend? Why?

THURSDAY

Read Proverbs 14:31; 22:9; 28:27.
Why do people avoid others? Why is it difficult to help someone who is needy? Have you ever been in need of something (lunch money, gas money, field trip money, etc.)? How did you deal with your need? How did it make you feel?

FRIDAY   **Read Proverbs 17:17; 18:24.**

List your three best friends. Why are they so important to you?
How loyal are you to them? Why are you loyal?

SATURDAY   **Read Proverbs 24:17-18; 25:21-22.**

Do you have any enemies? How easy is it to love your enemies?
Why should you love them?

SUNDAY   **Read John 13:34-35.**

Why is love so important? What can people tell about you by the way you
love others?

G

LARGE-GROUP OPENING:
Get everyone's attention. Make announcements. Open your session with a prayer. Read the LifePoint to the students.

Regarding last week's "Now What?" ask how placing the focus away from self felt, or what levels of pride students discovered in themselves.

 LifePoint

A kind and loving spirit is characteristic of a Christian's life. People see Christ in
you through the love and kindness you show others.

SMALL-GROUP TIME:
Instruct students to separate into smaller groups of 4-8, preferably in a circle configuration. Call on the mature student or adult leaders you recruited to facilitate each small group through the "Say What?" segment.

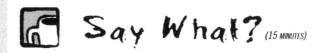 # Say What? *(15 MINUTES)*

Random Question of the Week:
Why do we refer to a "pair" of pants when it's only one item?

Group Experience: Pay It Forward

Give every student 15 round stickers and direct students to put their stickers on their hands. Inform students that they have five minutes to collect as many stickers from others as possible. Students can receive a sticker by doing something "kind" for another person. *(tying their shoe if it is untied, fixing their hair if it is messed up, fixing a wrinkled collar on a shirt, and so on. Encourage students to be as creative as they are kind).*

The rules are simple:
- You must allow someone to do a kind deed for you
- You must give someone a sticker for doing a kind deed
- You may not perform a kind deed for the person to whom you just gave a sticker

When time is up, ask the students to count their round stickers. Reward the person with the most stickers with a prize.

After the exercise, ask these follow-up questions:

1. Were people genuinely kind to you in this activity? How can you tell?

2. Was it easy to be kind to others? Why or why not?

3. As you think about your relationships with your friends, are you encouraged or discouraged? Are you kind to your friends on a regular basis?

4. If you were going to be stranded on a deserted island, would it be easy to find three people you wouldn't mind being "stranded" with? What character traits contribute to making this decision?

5. How important is genuine kindness in relationships?

So What? *(30 MINUTES)*

LARGE-GROUP TIME: Have the students turn to face the front for this teaching time. Be sure you can make eye contact with each student in the room. Encourage students to follow along and take notes in their student books.

Teaching Outline

I. Love and Kindness
  A. Love is always noticed
  B. Kindness requires refocusing your attention

II. Proverbs 12:25; 14:21,31; 17:17; 18:24; 20:6; 21:21; 22:9; 24:17-18; 25:21-22; 28:27

III. Generosity and Loyalty as Love
  A. God created the world to work "upside down" relative to the way we might think it should work
  B. Showing love and kindness isn't always what our world respects
  C. There are both earthly and spiritual benefits for showing kindness

IV. The Love of a Friend
  A. True friendship is a form of love
  B. A brother is born during difficult times

V. Loyalty and Trustworthiness
  A. Loyalty is rare these days
  B. Loyalty is a part of God's character

6

VI. Loving Strangers, Enemies, and People in Need
  A. Love of others runs from extreme to the other on our relational scales
  B. We love others—enemies, strangers, and the needy—because God does

TEACHING FOR THE LARGE GROUP: Share the "So What?" teaching with your students. You may modify it to meet your needs.

Be sure to highlight the underlined information which gives answers to the student book questions and fill-in-the-blanks (shown in the margins).

Love and Kindness

Being a true friend is difficult. It requires a good understanding of love and kindness. Both of these words appear simple on the surface. We have all experienced a friend's love at some point in our lives just as we have all been on the receiving end of someone else's genuine kindness. But how accurate is our definition of these terms?

When you walk through the door of the mall and someone holds the door open for you, what goes through your mind? Do you even notice this kind gesture? Chances are, unless you are used to living a life where people open doors for you on a regular basis, you notice the kindness others give to you. However, sometimes it so difficult to be kind in return because, in order to be kind, we must get rid of our own selfishness and begin to think less about ourselves and more about others.

Learning from the Bible

Learning from the Bible ...

Proverbs 12:25; 14:21, 31; 17:17; 18:24; 20:6; 21:21; 22:9; 24:17-18; 25:21-22; 28:27.

Anxiety in a man's heart weighs it down,
but a good word cheers it up.–Proverbs 12:25

The one who despises his neighbor sins,
but whoever shows kindness to the poor will
be happy.–Proverbs 14:21

The one who oppresses the poor insults their Maker,
but one who is kind to the needy honors Him.–Proverbs 14:31

A friend loves at all times,
and a brother is born for a difficult time.–Proverbs 17:17

A man with many friends may be harmed,
but there is a friend who stays closer than a brother.–Proverbs 18:24

Many a man proclaims his own loyalty,
but who can find a trustworthy man?–Proverbs 20:6

The one who pursues righteousness and faithful love
will find life, righteousness, and honor.–Proverbs 21:21

A generous person will be blessed,
for he shares his food with the poor.–Proverbs 22:9

Don't gloat when your enemy falls,
and don't let your heart rejoice when he stumbles,
or the LORD will see, be displeased,
and turn His wrath away from him.–Proverbs 24:17-18

If your enemy is hungry, give him food to eat,
and if he is thirsty, give him water to drink;

LARGE-GROUP TIME
CONTINUED:
This is the meat of the
teaching time. Remind
students to follow along
and take notes in their
student books.

As you share the
"So What?" information
with students, make
it your own. Use your
natural teaching style.
You may modify it with
your own perspectives
and teaching needs.
Emphasize the
underlined information,
which gives key points,
answers to the student
book questions or fill-in-
the-blanks in the (shown
in the margins).

❶ What are
some examples of
me-centered thinking
that prevent me from
showing kindness?

❷ What is the
relationship between
humility and love?

❸ What are some
earthly and heavenly
benefits to showing
love and kindness?

❹ What kind of
love gets the most
attention?

❺ What other kinds
of love are there?

for you will heap coals on his head,
and the LORD will reward you.—Proverbs 25:21-22

The one who gives to the poor
will not be in need,
but one who turns his eyes away
will receive many curses.—Proverbs 28:27

Generosity and Loyalty

The world God made would appear to be "upside down" relative to how we think it ought to be. There are many biblical examples of this "Upside Down Principle." One example is when Jesus says, "Whoever loses his life because of Me will find it" (Matt. 16:25). We try to cling to what is good for us (or at least what we think is good for us), but if we give ourselves up for God, we'll find something better than survival.

This upside down principle is also true of God's wisdom on love and kindness. The physical world, the world we live and breathe in, doesn't always ask for love and kindness. It certainly doesn't make it easy. We tend to look out for number one and this me-centered attitude is not easy to shed. For instance, ❶ a friend calls and needs help on a day you've planned to stay at home and play video games. Even if you decide to help, your initial urge is to resist. Or you've saved a little money for something special and a loved one has a financial crisis. If you don't help, you feel selfish and mean; if you do help, you regret losing your hard-earned cash. Our initial response to a situation is usually not kindness and love.

Developing humility is a lot like developing love and kindness. ❷ Humility is the attitude behind the action of love. A humble person sees other people as more important than himself. When we put that attitude into action we begin to show love and kindness.

Solomon teaches that someone who gives love and kindness benefits as much as the receiver does. ❸ There are earthly benefits to being loving and kind, like a pleasant feeling of friendliness and peace. There are also spiritual benefits, like God's reward for showing kindness to enemies, strangers, and people in need.

❹ Our culture points to romantic love as the ultimate experience. Yet, there are many other varieties of love. ❺ The affection we feel for family members and close friends is love. Benevolence (good will) toward others, even strangers, is also a kind of love. Leviticus 19:18 states, "Love your neighbor as yourself." Jesus restates this command as, "Whatever you want others to do for you, do also the same for them" (Matt. 7:12). The love we are to have for others is not primarily about emotion. It is about how we treat people. Love is an action.

The Love of a Friend

Proverbs 18:24 warns of someone with too many friends. The point of this insight is not that it is bad to be friendly. Rather, it is bad to be shallow. Some people never experience the kind of friends who stay "closer than a brother."

True friendship is a form of love. To lose a true friend hurts as much as losing family. A true friend gives and takes because love involves both needing and giving. That's why we spend so much time talking on the phone, the computer, and in person with our friends.

❻ According to Solomon, how can we recognize a true friend?

Hard times are a test of true friendship. Does a friend give comfort, stay close, or fade awkwardly away in a difficult time? ❻ Solomon says, "a brother is born for a difficult time" (Prov. 17:17). There is wisdom in this verse about how to be a good friend as well as how to recognize one. Loyalty and encouragement are marks of friendship.

Loyalty and Trustworthiness

Loyalty is an intense expression of love throughout Scripture. Consider Jonathan and David and how David mourned at Jonathan's loss. Or examine the story of Ruth and Naomi in the Book of Ruth. Then of course there is Jesus' loyalty to His friends and the disciples—not to mention the rest of us.

Loyalty is rare. Many promise it and claim to value it but let others down when a need arises (Prov. 20:6). There are many reasons—sometimes we're lazy or just tired. Sometimes we are really busy and sometimes we are less than passionate about our commitment to others. Loyalty requires a level of intention and effort. Like anything worth doing, being loyal takes a part of us—a part we voluntarily give up —and makes us more than we are.

❼ Loyal love is godly love.

Loyalty and faithfulness are inherent in God's character as well as ours as we reflect Him. We should never let a busy schedule or any other excuse keep us from being available to a friend who needs us. Loyalty is a part of loving God, and God forgives and keeps us even when we are not good friends to Him. ❼ Loyal love is godly love.

Loving Strangers, Enemies, and People in Need

Love and kindness certainly run the gamut of our relational scale. Friends and family are at one end of love. At the other end are strangers, enemies, and the profoundly needy. We love strangers and the poor to honor God (Prov. 14:31). ❽ A man may love a friend because he enjoys the love returned, but to love a stranger is to be selfless. There is no way to explain loving those we don't know apart of the love of Christ being within.

❽ Why is it especially praiseworthy to love strangers, enemies, and the needy?

We should love humanity because God does. In fact, God so loves humanity that He validated us through the ultimate sacrifice of His Son. Therefore, we are all valuable to Him by simply being human. So failing to feel love for others stands in contradiction to God's own heart (Prov. 14:31).

SMALL-GROUP TIME:
Use this time to help students begin to integrate the truth they've learned into their lives while they connect with other students in the group, the leaders, and with God.

After presenting the teaching material, ask students to divide back into small groups and discuss the "Do What?" questions. Small group facilitators should lead the discussions and set they tone by being open and honest in responding to each question.

 # Do What? *(15 MINUTES)*

Group Experience: ?

1. Would you say you have enough friends, not enough friends, or too many? Explain.

2. What makes being friends with someone easier? What makes loving others more difficult?

3. Why is it easier to love some people more than others? At what point do you quit trying to love someone else? Can people ever reach the point where they don't deserve our love?

4. How do you love people who are unlovable? Can you describe a time when you made a special attempt to love someone who did not act like they wanted to be loved?

5. How does loving others honor God?

LifePoint Review

Small-group facilitators should reinforce the LifePoint for this session. Make sure that student's questions are invited and addressed honestly.

A kind and loving spirit is characteristic of a Christian's life. People see Christ in you through the love and kindness you show others.

"Do" Points:

These "Do" Points will help you grab hold of this week's LifePoint. Be open and honest as you answer the questions within your small group.

1. Learn to recognize me-centered thinking. You'll be surprised where it pops up. **Where are the me-centered areas of your life?**

2. Choose to become a loyal person. Loyalty is not something that is reserved just for Bible characters or TV shows; it is something we should all pursue. **Are you loyal to your friends and the people you love?**

3. Develop ways to show kindness to others. God desires you to be a kind person. He wants to help you be kind to everyone, not just those who are easy to get along with. **How will you show kindness to someone that is difficult to get along with this week?**

Be sure to end your session by asking students to share prayer needs with one another, especially as they relate to issues brought up by today's session.

Prayer Connection:

This is the time to encourage, support, and pray for each other. Share prayer needs with the group, especially those related to forgiving those who have wronged you. Your group facilitator will close your time in prayer.

Prayer Needs:

Encourage students to list prayer needs for others in their books so they can pray for one another during the week. Assign a student coordinator in each small group to gather the group's requests and e-mail them to the group members.

now What?

Encourage students to dig a little deeper by completing a "Now What?" assignment before the next time you meet. Remind students about the "Get Ready" short daily Bible readings and related questions at the beginning of session 7.

Deepen your understanding of who God is and continue the journey you've begun today by choosing one of the following assignments to complete this week:

Option 1:

Read Matthew 5:43-48 daily for the next week. Make a list of your easy-to-love friends. Write down one or two reasons why you love each person on your list. Also, make a list of the difficult-to-love people in your life. Beside their names, write down one or two reasons why you have a difficult time showing them love and kindness. Spend time praying this week for your entire list, the people you love as well as those you have trouble loving. Let God speak to your heart.

Option 2:

Spend some time with a friend this week. Tell him the things that you appreciate about him. Don't just focus on the fun things that you do together. Take the time to let her know WHY you appreciate her. When you let people know you think about them and are concerned about them, you strengthen the bridge of friendship.

6

Bible Reference notes

Use these notes to deepen your understanding as you study the Bible on your own:

Proverbs 14:21

despises. Holds in contempt, belittles, ridicules. God held the whole nation responsible for their poor neighbors.

Proverbs 14:31

God is a protector of the poor (22:22-23). Our actions toward the poor reflect our attitude toward God.

Proverbs 24:17-18

gloat. An attitude of superiority. God detests this attitude—even when we gloat over adversaries.

Proverbs 25:21

If your enemy. Jesus taught this in Luke 6:27-31.

Proverbs 25:22

heap coals. When a fire went out, the homeowner would often borrow burning coals from a neighbor to start the fire again. In Egyptian culture carrying burning coals on one's head was a ritual of repentance. (See also Romans 12:20.)

NOTES

Session

7

·HONESTLY SPEAKING

CoNNecĥioNs Prep

MAIN LIFEPOINT:

God takes honesty very seriously. We do not have the right to change the truth, bend the truth, or omit the truth for our own benefit. God honors honesty and despises lying.

To reinforce the LifePoint, leaders and small-group facilitators should understand the following more detailed CheckPoints and "Do" Points.

BIBLE STUDY CHECKPOINTS:

· Understand how seriously God views dishonesty
· Develop faith in God's blessings for those that live honestly
· Deepen a desire to live at peace with God through being honest

LIFE CHANGE "DO" POINTS:

· Realize God takes honesty very seriously
· Focus on the truth
· Recognize the advantages of being honest

PREPARATION:

☐ Review the leader book for this session and prepare your teaching.
☐ Determine how you will subdivide students into small discussion groups.
☐ Recruit mature students or adults as small-group facilitators. Be sure these facilitators plan to attend.

REQUIRED SUPPLIES:

☐ *Proverbs: Uncommon Sense* leader books for each group facilitator
☐ *Proverbs: Uncommon Sense* student books for each student
☐ Pens or pencils for each student
☐ Index cards for each student

Get Ready

This "Get Ready" section is primarily for the students, but leaders and facilitators will benefit from these devotionals as well.

Read one of these short Bible passages each day and spend a few minutes wrapping your brain around it. Be sure to jot down any insights you discover.

MONDAY

Read Proverbs 19:1; 28:6.

What is integrity? Why is it important in a Christian's life? Who is someone you know with integrity? How do they demonstrate it?

TUESDAY

Read Psalm 15:1-5.

Which actions in this psalm surprise you? How do you feel when you read a list like this? How would you rate yourself according to this list? How many people do you know who are qualified to live on "God's Holy Mountain?"

WEDNESDAY

Read Proverbs 20:17; 21:6.

Have you ever been tempted to lie in order to succeed? Did you follow through on the temptation? What do these passages say about lying in order to gain fortune?

THURSDAY

Read Proverbs 11:20; 12:22.

How would you rate your own honesty? How important is honesty to God? Why? Spend some time talking to God honestly about your life today.

FRIDAY

Read Proverbs 13:6.

What is righteousness? What is wickedness? List some examples of each. Evaluate your own life. Which characteristic better describes you and your lifestyle? Explain.

SATURDAY

Read Proverbs 14:25; 19:28.

How important is it for someone to be an honest witness? Why do you think God feels so strongly against false witnesses?

SUNDAY

Read Psalm 26:1-3.

What do you think about David's prayer? Could you pray like this? In your own words, re-write David's prayer from your point of view.

LARGE-GROUP OPENING:
Get everyone's attention.
Make announcements.
Open your session with a prayer. Read the LifePoint to the students.

Ask what revelations last week's "Now What?" challenges brought.

 LifePoint

God takes honesty very seriously. We do not have the right to change the truth, bend the truth, or omit the truth for our own benefit. God honors honesty and despises lying.

SMALL-GROUP TIME:
Instruct students to separate into smaller groups of 4-8, preferably in a circle configuration. Call on the mature student or adult leaders you recruited to facilitate each small group through this "Say What?" segment.

Say What? *(15 MINUTES)*

Random Question of the Week:

Why are the vowels in the words GOOD and FOOD pronounced differently?

Group Experience: Two Truths and a Lie

Play a round of "Two truths and a lie." Give the students an index card and instruct them not to put their names on it. Have each student write down three statements about themselves. Instruct them to list two true statements and one lie about themselves. Encourage them to be creative and think of facts about themselves that even their friends don't know. When the students are finished, collect their cards. Read the three statements on each index card aloud. Give the students a chance to guess who they think wrote the statements and which statements are true and which statement is false.

After the exercise, ask these follow-up questions:

1. Which was more difficult, knowing who wrote the statements or which statement was a lie? Why?

2. How difficult was it for you to invent a lie? Did you try to create a "believable" lie? Why do you think people lie?

3. Describe a time in your life when you told a lie and got caught. How did you feel? Why did you choose to lie? What was the motivation?

 # So What? *(30 MINUTES)*

LARGE-GROUP TIME:
Have the students turn
to face the front for
this teaching time. Be
sure you can make
eye contact with each
student in the room.
Encourage students to
follow along and take
notes in their student
books.

Share the "So What?"
information with your
large group of students.
You may modify it with
your own perspectives
and teaching needs.
Be sure to highlight the
underlined information
which gives answers
to the student book
questions and fill-in-
the-blanks (shown in
the margins).

Teaching Outline

I. Honesty
    A. Honesty is something we desire, but struggle with
    B. Honesty is something we all demand but few possess

II. Proverbs 11:20; 12:22; 13:6; 14:25; 19:1,28; 20:17; 21:6; 28:6

III. Types of Dishonesty
    A. The Lord detests dishonesty
    B. Other common forms of dishonesty include slander (insults), false joy (being fake), and cheating
    C. We can be dishonest in our answers and commitments with Christians to pray for them

IV. Lying
    A. Lying breaks confidence in relationships
    B. Being lied to is difficult to overcome

V. Stealing
    A. Stealing is selfish
    B. Righteousness is selflessness
    C. Stealing brings with it feelings of insecurity and guilt

VI. Cheating
    A. Cheating is deceiving someone to believe you are someone you are not
    B. Cheating requires constant maintenance to conceal your true identity
    C. Cheating brings emptiness

VII. Slandering
    A. Slandering isn't limited to the courtroom
    B. We slander when we speak an untruth about someone
    C. Slander destroys trust between friends
    D. An honest person saves others' lives

VIII. Integrity and Blamelessness

A. Blameless integrity is the opposite of dishonesty

B. Integrity commands respect, even from the immoral

C. Friends desire integrity

D. God does not have to discipline a person who has integrity

**TEACHING FOR THE
LARGE GROUP:**
Share the "So What?"
teaching with your
students. You may
modify it to meet your
needs.

Be sure to highlight
the underlined
information, which
gives answers to the
student book questions
and fill-in-the-blanks
(shown in the margins).

Honesty

Honesty is something followers of Christ desire. We strive to be known as honest people, and we desire honest friends. Yet, we are tempted daily to lie. Diogenes the Cynic, a traveling Greek philosopher, used to go out at night carrying a lamp as if he was looking for something. People would ask him what he was looking for. With a straight face he would look them in the eye and answer, "An honest man!"

Honesty is something we all demand but few possess completely. Dishonesty is rampant; few are untouched by it. From little white lies, to cheating on tests, to lying in order to stay out of trouble, most people have lied—again and again and again. A recent survey found that while 92 percent of Christian students believe it is wrong to copy someone else's homework, 55 percent admit to doing it (*Christianity Today*, "Campus Life," November/December 1999). So even if we say lying is wrong and criticize others for doing it, dishonesty is a real part of our lives.

In this week's session, we will learn how God values honest lips and honest hearts. We will be challenged to view cheating or forgetting to follow through on promises as more serious than commonly thought. Finally, we will be motivated to seek God's peace and blessing through an honest life.

Learning from the Bible

Before the session,
enlist a student to read

Proverbs 11:20; 12:22;
13:6; 14:25; 19:1,28;
20:17; 21:6; 28:6.

*Those with twisted minds are detestable to the LORD,
but those with blameless conduct are His delight.—Proverbs 11:20*

*Lying lips are detestable to the LORD,
but faithful people are His delight.—Proverbs 12:22*

*Righteousness guards people of integrity,
but wickedness undermines the sinner.—Proverbs 13:6*

LARGE-GROUP TIME
CONTINUED:
This is the meat of the
teaching time. Remind
students to follow along
and take notes in their
student books.

As you share the
"So What?" information
with students, make
it your own. Use your
natural teaching style.

Emphasize underlined
information, which gives
key points, answers to
the student book
questions or fill-in-the-
blanks in the (shown in
the margins).

A truthful witness rescues lives,
but one who utters lies is deceitful.—Proverbs 14:25

Better a poor man who walks in integrity
than someone who has deceitful lips and is a fool.—Proverbs 19:1

A worthless witness mocks justice,
and a wicked mouth swallows iniquity.—Proverbs 19:28

Food gained by fraud is sweet to a man,
but afterwards his mouth is full of gravel.—Proverbs 20:17

Making a fortune through a lying tongue
is a vanishing mist, a pursuit of death.—Proverbs 21:6

Better a poor man who lives with integrity
than a rich man who distorts right and wrong.—Proverbs 28:6

Types of Dishonesty

❶ What else does God detest besides dishonesty?

The Lord detests dishonesty. ❶ The biblical word used for *detests* is the same word used for God's attitude toward extreme sexual sin in Leviticus 18 (see vv. 22, 26-27,29-30), toward idolatry in Deuteronomy 7:25, and toward insincere worship in Isaiah 1:13. Dishonesty is no minor sin. It is not a matter of, "Everyone is doing it." God created the world with words. How we use words matters to Him. When we twist words by lying, deceiving, and hiding the truth, we are abusing the power of words given to us by God. Dishonesty always has and will continue to be sin.

❷ What is a common, yet dishonest practice about our promises to pray?

Several types of dishonesty flood the Christian culture. ❷ Christians frequently say, "Will you pray for us? We're facing this really tough situation." We nod our heads or even verbalize, "Sure, I'll pray," in response knowing that we won't remember what they told us in ten minutes. Many times, the people asking us to pray don't even really expect us to. It's more like a religious way of sharing news than a sincere request to be lifted before the Father.

❸ List some types of dishonesty.

❸ Other common forms of dishonesty include slander (insults), false joy (being fake), and cheating. We slander others by repeating unproven gossip. We express false joy when we let our religious talk obscure the reality of the pain in our lives. We cheat because we value self-gain over God's favor in our lives.

④ What two contrasts are made in Proverbs 11:20?

Solomon describes the contrast between honesty and dishonesty in Proverbs 11:20. He says that **④ a person can have blameless conduct or a twisted mind.** The twisted mind is literally a distorted heart. The heart is the center of the emotions, the mind, and the will. To have a distorted heart is to be twisted at the core. Dishonesty is a symptom of a soul that is not right. On the other hand, blameless conduct is literally the perfect way or a blameless road. A person who walks in blamelessness cannot be faulted in his or her ways. His path is straight.

Lying

⑤ According to Proverbs 12:22, why are lies taken so personally?

Lying is the most obvious kind of dishonesty. Just as the twisted mind is detestable to God, so are lying lips (Prov. 12:22). Lying is unfaithfulness. It is breaking faith with the person to whom you are lying. **⑤ This explains why lies hurt so much when they are discovered. People put faith in you when they hear you speak. When your deception is discovered, that faith is broken and people are hurt. Lying is a common sin, but it isn't easily forgiven.** Once you've broken someone's trust, you've lost your integrity, and integrity is very difficult to regain. It's hard to forget that someone has lied to you. It is like sticking duct tape to a piece of construction paper and then trying to remove it without damaging the paper; it's very difficult to do. The pain that lying creates takes time and tremendous effort to overcome, so honesty from the beginning is the best option.

Stealing

Stealing is another form of dishonesty. In a Jewish writing called the Mishnah, a rabbi speaks of three kinds of people. The first person says, "What's mine is mine and what's yours is mine." The second says, "What's mine is mine and what's yours is yours." The third, the most righteous, says, "What's mine is yours and what's yours is yours."

⑥ How does stolen food taste like gravel (Prov. 20:17)?

Stealing is a sin of selfishness. The righteous are selfless. They would rather give away than take. Their minds are not totally fixed on themselves. The thief who thinks stealing will better his or her life often finds bitterness. The stolen food ends up tasting like gravel (Prov. 20:17). **⑥ A thief is always looking over his shoulder wondering, "Are my victims coming after me?" There are many ways in which crime does not pay. Fear, insecurity, and guilt are just few of its results.**

Cheating

Cheating is another form of stealing. It is success by fraud. A cheater makes better grades by deceiving people and scores better on tests by deception. A cheater looks better than he or she really is but always runs the risk of being found out to be a fraud. Cheaters constantly have to maintain the façade of whom they are pretending to be.

❼ How is wealth
obtained by fraud like
a vanishing mist
(Prov. 21:6)?

Solomon warns that wealth obtained by fraud is a vanishing mist (Prov. 21:6). ❼ Many times fraudulent wealth is taken away or becomes impossible to enjoy because it is never enough to satisfy the cheater. Cheating is empty, like an immaculate house that is beautiful on the outside but filled with wicked hearts on the inside.

Slandering

❽ How can you be
a false witness and
not be in a courtroom
(Prov. 19:29)?

The ninth commandment says, "Do not give false testimony against your neighbor" (Ex. 20:16). Many people feel slander is not a sin they would ever commit because it applies only to the courtroom. ❽ In reality, anytime you repeat unproven gossip about someone, even if you do not know if the gossip is true, you are slandering. Slander is saying something about someone that is not true. If you do not know something to be true, but you repeat it anyway, you are slandering. Slander is something that is also difficult to undo. When you speak untruth about someone, it tears down trust and confidence in you as well.

❾ How does a truthful
witness save lives
(Prov. 14:25)?

Solomon says that a truthful witness saves lives (Prov. 14:25). ❾ The truth in this statement is easy to see. A person's reputation is invaluable. One slanderous comment can ruin a person's reputation forever. When you are talking about someone else, always remember that you hold that person's reputation in your hand. Do not mock justice, for God values it highly (Prov. 19:28). God calls someone who mocks justice "worthless."

Integrity and Blamelessness

The ugliness of dishonesty should drive us to a life of blameless integrity. Integrity is so rare and sought after that it is no wonder Diogenes the Cynic wandered the streets of ancient Greece searching for an honest man. Integrity is a shield for the righteous (Prov. 13:6). Even an immoral teacher will ultimately respect students who have integrity. Friends seek out friends who will be straight with them, and God does not have to discipline an honest person.

Even though cheating, lying, stealing, and slandering may seem to get a person ahead in life, it is better to be poor and blameless (Prov. 19:1). Peace of mind and peace with other people is more valuable. Once you have sold out to money over integrity, you can never fully gain your integrity back. It vanishes like the mist.

Remember these words from Philippians: "My eager expectation and hope is that I will not be ashamed about anything, but that now as always, with all boldness, Christ will be highly honored in my body, whether by life or by death. For me, living is Christ and dying is gain" (Phil. 1:20-21). Let's honor Christ by living a blameless life.

SMALL-GROUP TIME:
Use this time to help students begin to integrate the truth they've learned into their lives while they connect with other students in the group, the leaders, and with God.

After presenting the teaching material, ask students to divide back into small groups and discuss the "Do What?" questions. Small group facilitators should lead the discussions and set they tone by being open and honest in responding to each question.

 # Do What? *(15 MINUTES)*

1. Where are you living right now in terms of honesty? Check one.
   ☐ In the light. Honesty is very important to me.
   ☐ In the shade. I admit I color the truth to suit myself, though I'm basically honest.
   ☐ In the half-light. I have benefited from dishonesty, but I've turned my life around.
   ☐ In the shifting shadows. I'm usually honest, but sometimes I can tell a HUGE lie—especially if it helps me get what I want and deserve!
   ☐ In the dark! I need to quit cheating and lying right now.
   ☐ Other: _____

2. Complete this sentence: "Dishonesty is a serious sin because . . ."

3. What thought inspires you the most to be honest? Check one.
   ☐ Lying is a sin others find hard to forgive.
   ☐ Cheaters and liars don't get away with it forever.
   ☐ God delights in the blameless.
   ☐ God detests lying lips.
   ☐ God despises all dishonesty—big or small.
   ☐ Other: _____

4. How can God help you become a more honest person?

5. How difficult is it for you to recognize dishonesty in others? How do you feel when you are dishonest with others? Do you feel like they know you are being dishonest? Why?

 # LifePoint Review

God takes honesty very seriously. We do not have the right to change the truth, bend the truth, or omit the truth for our own benefit. God honors honesty and despises lying.

"Do" Points:

These "Do" Points will help you grab hold of this week's LifePoint. Be open and honest as you answer the questions within your small group.

1. <u>Realize God takes honesty very seriously.</u> When we are dishonest with our words and our actions, a single person may not catch us, but God knows what we are doing at all times (Ps. 139).
Think of an example from the Bible that proves that God takes dishonesty seriously.

2. <u>Focus on the truth.</u> Even though you might be tempted to present yourself as the hero in your stories, you don't have to. God knows the real you, and others have the right to know you too. Changing the truth to make yourself look better is wrong.
What keeps you from constantly telling the truth?

3. <u>Recognize the advantages of being honest.</u> When you are honest, God is pleased, and He delights in you. Being honest brings blessings and helps you avoid discipline from God.
Do you know someone who is honest? What is his or her life like?

Be sure to end your session by asking students to share prayer needs with one another, especially as they relate to issues brought up by today's session.

Encourage students to list prayer needs for others in their books so they can pray for one another during the week. Assign a student coordinator in each small group to gather the group's requests and e-mail them to the group members.

Encourage students to dig a little deeper by completing a "Now What" assignment before the next time you meet. Remind students about the "Get Ready" short daily Bible readings and related questions at the beginning of session 8.

Prayer Connection:

This is the time to encourage, support, and pray for each other in our journeys to trust God and seek out real and personal encounters with Him.

Share prayer needs with the group, especially those related to hearing from and responding to God. Your group facilitator will close your time in prayer.

Prayer Needs:

 # now What?

Deepen your understanding of who God is and continue the journey you've begun today by choosing one of the following assignments to complete this week:

Option 1:
Pay attention to the words you say this week. When you are tempted to lie, take a moment to pause before you speak. Why are you choosing to lie? Are you trying to look good in front of your friends? Are you trying to get something you don't deserve? Are you trying to be included by a group of people? As you begin to recognize when you are tempted to lie, you will be able to avoid those situations. Before next week, write a paragraph detailing what you have found out about yourself when you are tempted to lie.

Option 2:
Meditate on and memorize Proverbs 11:20 this week. Take time daily to evaluate your honesty. As you look at your life, journal about a time when you lied and describe how you feel about that now.

Bible Reference Notes

Use these notes to deepen your understanding as you study the Bible on your own:

Proverbs 14:25   *witness.* A witness has the power to either save life or destroy it through deceitful testimony.

Proverbs 19:28   *swallows.* The practice of evil is a delight to the wicked.

Proverbs 20:17   *gravel.* This is an apt picture of the long-term consequences of sin. At first, getting away with something is sweet, but in the end we are left with the remains of our broken character.

NOTES

Session

8

CORRECT ME IF I'M WRONG

Connections Prep

MAIN LIFEPOINT: Learning to accept correction is a sign of maturity in the life of a Christian. God uses many forms of correction to get our attention. Being corrected is not fun, but it is a vital part of our spiritual growth.

To reinforce the LifePoint, leaders and small-group facilitators should understand the following more detailed CheckPoints and "Do" Points.

BIBLE STUDY CHECKPOINTS:
- Understand the difficulty and the reward of receiving correction
- Accept correction and discipline from our family and friends
- Learn from all types of correction (including anger and insults)

LIFE CHANGE "DO" POINTS:
- Make a list of frequent criticisms you hear about yourself
- Spend time with a friend who sharpens you spiritually this week
- Meditate on and memorize Proverbs 12:1

PREPARATION:
- ☐ Review the leader book for this session and prepare your teaching.
- ☐ Determine how you will subdivide students into small discussion groups.
- ☐ Recruit mature students or adults as small-group facilitators. Be sure these facilitators plan to attend.

REQUIRED SUPPLIES:
- ☐ *Proverbs: Uncommon Sense* leader books for each group facilitator
- ☐ *Proverbs: Uncommon Sense* student books for each student
- ☐ Pens or pencils for each student
- ☐ Index card for each student

 # Get Ready

Read one of these short Bible passages each day and spend a few minutes wrapping your brain around it. Be sure to jot down any insights you discover.

MONDAY   **Read Proverbs 13:13.**
Why is it difficult to listen to instructions and respect commands? Who is the one person it is hardest for you to take commands or correction from? Why?

TUESDAY   **Read Proverbs 13:18; 19:20.**
What life advice have you ignored? Why did you ignore it? What was the outcome? What advice or discipline has helped you most in your life? What advice or discipline has hurt you the most?

WEDNESDAY   **Read Proverbs 12:1; 15:32.**
How are instruction and knowledge related? Whose advice do you cherish the most? What characteristics does this person possess that make you want to listen and follow them?

THURSDAY   **Read Proverbs 21:11.**
What life lessons are you learning right now? What lesson have you learned because of discipline or punishment? Are you glad you learned it?

FRIDAY   **Read Proverbs 27:5-6; 28:23.**

Have you ever been corrected by a friend? How did it make you feel? Were you initially angry with them? How did you overcome your anger? How is your relationship with that friend now?

SATURDAY   **Read Proverbs 27:17.**

Who sharpens your life? If you don't have someone that is sharpening you, who could you approach about assuming that position in your life? What are the benefits of a sharpened life?

SUNDAY   **Read Proverbs 13:24; 29:17.**

How do your parents discipline you? How will you discipline your children? Why is discipline important?

8

LARGE-GROUP OPENING:
Get everyone's attention. Make announcements. Open your session with a prayer. Read the LifePoint to the students.

Ask about last week's "Now What?" activities. Ask the students if they were tempted to lie during the week. If time permits, spend a couple of minutes listening to the response.

 LifePoint

Learning to accept correction is a sign of maturity in the life of a Christian. God uses many forms of correction to get our attention. Being corrected is not fun, but it is a vital part of our spiritual growth.

SMALL-GROUP TIME:
Instruct students to separate into smaller groups of 4-8, preferably in a circle configuration. Call on the mature student or adult leaders you recruited to facilitate each small group through this "Say What?" segment.

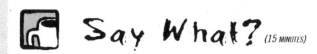 Say What? *(15 MINUTES)*

Random Question of the Week:
What was the best thing BEFORE sliced bread?

Group Experience: Rock, Paper, Scissors

Give each student an index card and a pencil. Tell them you are going to play a game of "rock, paper, scissors," and they will need a partner. After they've chosen their partners, have them create one rule for the game and write it on their index card (encourage them to be creative and make a rule that will benefit them). For instance, if one student's rule is whoever is wearing black tennis shoes automatically wins, anyone that is wearing black tennis shoes wins the game. When everyone is finished writing their rules, collect the cards. Pull out one rule and use it to judge the first round of "rock, paper, scissors," but don't tell the students what the rule is. Use a new rule for each round. Even though you're playing "rock, paper, scissors"—it doesn't matter because no one knows the rules. In the event of a tie, the actual game of "rock, paper, scissors" will count. Have students switch partners after each round. Continue to play this way until you have used all of the rules.

When the game is over, ask the following questions:

1. How difficult was it to play a game when the rules were unknown? Why is it important to know the rules before you begin?

2. How difficult was it when the rules kept changing? What made the game more difficult, not knowing the rules or knowing the rules were always changing?

3. Who benefited from the rules? What is the advantage of everyone getting to make up their own rules? Why is it important to have one set of rules that everyone uses? Does conflict arise when you don't know what to expect?

LARGE-GROUP TIME:
Have the students turn
to face the front for
this teaching time. Be
sure you can make eye
contact with each student
in the room. Encourage
students to follow along
and take notes in their
student books.

Share the "So What?"
information with your
large group of students.
You may modify it with
your own perspectives
and teaching needs.
Be sure to highlight the
underlined information
which gives answers
to the student book
questions and fill-in-
the-blanks (shown in
the margins).

So What? *(30 MINUTES)*

Teaching Outline

I. Truth in Discipline
A. Correction is necessary
B. Correction is not easy to accept
C. We never outgrow discipline

II. Proverbs 12:1; 13:13,18,24; 15:32; 19:20; 21:11; 27:5-6,17; 28:23; 29:1

III. Ignoring Correction Is Foolish
A. There is a penalty for resisting criticism
B. Immature people repeat the same mistakes
C. Consequences come from not learning from mistakes

IV. Correction is the Path to Learning
A. We can learn from the reactions of others
B. A wise person cares more about knowledge than pride (Prov. 12:1)
C. Correction is for everyone

V. Discipline and Correction from Parents
A. Your parents are called by God to train you
B. A disciplined child lives a better life
C. Parents are called to be a trainer, not a friend

VI. Discipline and Correction from Friends and Family Members
A. It is difficult to hear criticism from people we're close to
B. We should not be afraid to accept criticism from loved ones
C. Wise people seek honest people who can sharpen their lives

VII. The Habit of Listening
A. Listen to what others say
B. Discern if there is truth in the criticism
C. Pride is your enemy, not your friend

8

VIII. Pruning

A. Pruning helps expose the good fruit in our lives

B. God can use anyone to prune us, even rude people

C. Correction will improve our lives

TEACHING FOR THE LARGE GROUP:

❶ What is one example of someone who needs correction?

❷ Why do we resent correction?

❸ Why does accepting correction seem particularly difficult?

Before the session, enlist a student to read Proverbs 12:1; 13:13, 18,24; 15:32; 19:20; 21:11; 27:5-6,17; 28:23; 29:17.

Truth in Criticism

❶ In the grocery store line, a child throws a tantrum over something his mom won't buy. You want to ask the parent, "Don't you discipline your kid?" ❶ In the locker room at school, a friend rolls her eyes as she tells you about a critical teacher. As she explains her teacher's comment, you know there is truth to it. Yet, she indicates she has no plan to accept it, and she expects you to back her up. ❶ While driving home, your parents say you've been spending too much money lately. You have a job, and you feel your anger rise. You think, *It's my money. I'll spend it if I want to!*

Discipline and correction are about as fun as going to the dentist. ❷ The reason we hate being corrected is pride. We want to be the authority in our life, we wave the "You're not the boss of me" banner, and we resent anyone else stepping in. Teenagers are notorious for despising correction and discipline—and we've all been teenagers. ❸ You are learning to think independently, and you feel like you have earned the right to make some mistakes. Many times, though, when a person offers you unwanted advice, correction, or discipline, there is usually some truth to it. The person may have no real authority in our lives, but truth does, and truth ultimately comes from God. And if we fail to address the truth, we pay the consequences.

Learning from the Bible

Whoever loves instruction loves knowledge,
but one who hates correction is stupid.–Proverbs 12:1

The one who has contempt for instruction will pay the penalty,
but the one who respects a command will be rewarded.–Proverbs 13:13

Poverty and disgrace come to those who ignore instruction,
but the one who accepts rebuke will be honored.–Proverbs 13:18

The one who will not use the rod hates his son,
but the one who loves him disciplines him diligently.—Proverbs 13:24

Anyone who ignores instruction despises himself,
but whoever listens to correction acquires good sense.—Proverbs 15:32

Listen to counsel and receive instruction
so that you may be wise in later life.—Proverbs 19:20

When a mocker is punished, the inexperienced become wiser; when one teaches a wise
man, he acquires knowledge.—Proverbs 21:11

Better an open reprimand
than concealed love.
The wounds of a friend are trustworthy,
but the kisses of an enemy are excessive.—Proverbs 27:5-6

Iron sharpens iron,
and one man sharpens another.—Proverbs 27:17

One who rebukes a person will later find more favor
than one who flatters with his tongue.—Proverbs 28:23

Discipline your son, and he will give you comfort;
he will also give you delight.—Proverbs 29:17

LARGE-GROUP TIME CONTINUED:
This is the meat of the teaching time. Remind students to follow along and take notes in their student books.

As you share the "So What?" information with students, make it your own.

Emphasize underlined information, which gives answers to the student book questions or fill-in-the-blanks in the (shown in the margins).

Ignoring Correction Is Foolish

There are three kinds of people in the world: those who have made mistakes, those who are making a mistake right now, and those who will soon make a mistake. Accepting discipline and correction is a part of being humble. People who are too proud to learn from mistakes and advice do not grow. Solomon says, "The one who rejects correction goes astray" (Prov. 10:17). Since we are not immune to mistakes, we should not be immune to criticism.

❹ What does Solomon warn will happen if we resist instruction?

❹ <u>Solomon warns us that we will pay a penalty for resisting instruction</u> (Prov. 13:13). If we don't change our ways, our critic's warnings may very well happen. Pride is usually what stands in our way. Proverbs 13:18 warns us that the path of pride leads to poverty and disgrace. Immature people keep making the same mistakes instead of learning from them. The consequences of resisting correction are often serious, and the pain usually comes in knowing they could have been avoided. The one who is too proud to learn from criticism unwittingly hates himself (Prov. 15:32). When we fail to learn from correction, we fall.

Correction Is the Path to Learning

We don't have to hate ourselves by rejecting correction. Instead, we can have good sense (Prov. 15:32). We can learn that even when people criticize us from bad motives, there is often truth in what they say. A wise person cares more about knowledge than pride (Prov. 12:1). When you make people angry, ask yourself why that is happening. When someone is rude to you, consider if you provoked it. Learn from your mistakes. Even rude, angry people may have something to teach us. We should learn from life's lessons and opportunities instead of rejecting them because they hurt.

❺ When it comes to correction, how are wise people different from foolish?

❺ <u>Don't think correction is only for fools. When a fool receives instruction, a simple person learns a simple lesson; when a wise man receives correction, a deep person learns a deep lesson (Prov. 21:11).</u> It may take time, but someone in the habit of listening will eventually become wise (Prov. 19:20).

Discipline and Correction from Parents

It is important to receive correction—especially from parents. The most important place for discipline and correction to occur is within the home. Uncorrected children follow their sinful desires when desires go unchecked and end up being punished instead by life.

In Proverbs 22:6, parents are directed to train their children. This is the same word that is used when referring to training a horse. Think about a wild horse. It is not easily led. It resists every instruction and will even pull away from the most experienced rider. In order for a horse to be trained, the trainer must endure long sessions of a battle of wills. If you have ever ridden a horse, you have benefited from the hard work of someone not willing to give up when the going got tough. In the same way, parents can't give up just because a child kicks, screams, or yells.

❻ What is one role your parents are to play in your life?

❻ <u>Your parents are called to be your trainer, not your friend, because they are preparing you for life away from home.</u>

❼ A disciplined child lives a better life. He learns that crying, begging, and raging will not get him what he wants. He also learns to respect authority, tell the truth, respect others, and respect property. A disciplined child is also a benefit to his parents (Prov. 29:17). Gaining wisdom through discipline doesn't stop when you reach a certain age. You will always be able to learn from others. **❼** So the next time your parents discipline you, remember that they are doing so because God instructs them to and because they love you. They want to see you become the person God created you to be.

❼ Give two reasons why your parents discipline you.

Discipline and Correction from Friends and Family Members

Sometimes the hardest people to receive correction from are those we love the most. Good friends or close family can hurt us when they correct us because they know us best. Yet, we should listen to their opinions more than anyone else's except God. Proverbs 27:5 states that it is better to be loved and criticized than not to have been loved at all. **❽** When a loved one bluntly criticizes us, we should be thankful for his or her love. And in the courage of a friend's wise anger, there is love (Prov. 27:6).

❽ Why should we listen to correction from family members or friends?

Likewise, we should not be afraid to correct a loved one. In the end, he will respect us more than he will appreciate a flatterer (Prov. 28:23). A flatterer tells people what they want to hear. Someone asks, "Am I gaining weight?" "No," the flatterer responds, "You're looking great." Eventually a person wishes for a friend whose honesty helps him to avoid the weight gain at the beginning. Wise people seek friends with whom they can be honest and who will be honest with them. Honest friends are like iron to iron; equals who sharpen each other (Prov. 27:17). A friend who sharpens you is a friend for life.

The Habit of Listening

❾ Like many other aspects of wisdom, heeding correction is a habit. Learn to listen and care about what others say. Listen especially for criticism. Consider it fertilizer for your character and spiritual growth. Recognize that pride is your enemy, not your friend. Over time, you will notice that you get criticized less and less as you become wise.

❾ What is a good habit that we can form to help us grow in wisdom?

Pruning

Discipline can be compared to pruning a tree or vine. **❿** Too much pruning can kill a plant, so pruning does hurt. Yet, a vine-grower who wants many sweet grapes will prune his vines to mere stumps. It is the new wood that produces good fruit. God uses this image to describe the way He disciplines us. "He prunes every branch that produces fruit so that it will produce more fruit" (John 15:2).

❿ How is discipline like pruning?

God uses people to do some of the pruning. We might be pruned by an angry person who insults us or by a loved one who offers correction to show us we are wrong. When we accept discipline and correction, we become wise.

⓫ List three ways our lives would be different if we welcomed correction.

How would life be different if we welcomed correction? ⓫ <u>First, we would listen more to other people. Second, we would argue less. Third, we would recognize the difference between untrue criticism and true correction. Finally, we would improve our character and manner of dealing with people from the lessons we learned.</u>

SMALL-GROUP TIME:
Use this time to help students begin to integrate the truth they've learned into their lives while they connect with the other students in the group, the leaders, and with God.

Ask students to divide back into small groups and discuss the "Do What?" questions. Small-group facilitators should lead the discussions and set the model by connecting with the students.

 # Do What? *(15 MINUTES)*

1. Tell the story of a time when someone corrected you in public and embarrassed you. How did it make you feel? Why?

2. Identify each example of correction below as wise or foolish.

wise   foolish

☐ ☐ Honking and shouting to another driver to slow down and be careful

☐ ☐ Writing a note to a waitress explaining why she got a low tip

☐ ☐ Getting grounded for borrowing the car without permission

☐ ☐ Explaining to an employee that he eventually will be fired if he cannot smile and speak politely to customers

☐ ☐ Correcting a stranger who steps on your foot carelessly

☐ ☐ Telling an angry person to "calm down and get a grip"

3. How well do you receive correction? Check one.
   ☐ I'd rather visit the dentist and drill my own mouth.
   ☐ I enjoy correction because I like returning the criticism.
   ☐ I don't enjoy correction, and I often respond with anger or an insult.
   ☐ I can take it from a friend but not from a stranger.
   ☐ I can take it from a stranger but not from a friend.
   ☐ Other: _____

4. What would help you to receive correction more gracefully? Check one.
   ☐ Only brain surgery would help me!
   ☐ If I prayed for and studied God's wisdom on humility.
   ☐ If I learned to separate the anger from the truth of the criticism.
   ☐ If I learned to listen more and think less about what to say in return.
   ☐ Other: _____

LifePoint Review

Small-group facilitators should reinforce the LifePoint for this session. Make sure that student's questions are invited and addressed honestly.

Learning to accept correction is a sign of maturity in the life of a Christian. God uses many forms of correction to get our attention. Being corrected is not fun, but it is a vital part of our spiritual growth.

"Do" Points:

These "Do" Points will help you grab hold of this week's LifePoint. Make an effort to connect with each other as you discuss the questions within your small group.

1. <u>Make a list of frequent criticisms you hear about yourself.</u> Write *true* or *false* beside each criticism. Explain how each criticism is true or false. For example, if you have heard that you don't make good use of your talent, you might put, "I need to be more focused and intentional" in the true column. In the false column you might write, "I am a passionate person who uses his gifts."
Pray for God to guide you to grow in the areas in which people criticize you.

2. <u>Spend time with a friend who sharpens you spiritually this week.</u> When you want to get better at sports, music, or school you take lessons. Imagine how much improvement your life could have if you found a spiritual tutor. Let your friend know you've been thinking about Proverbs 27:17 and your friendship.
Discuss ways you've helped each other grow in the past and talk about ways you might be able to help each other in the future. Agree to be receptive to correction.

Be sure to end your session by asking students to share prayer needs with one another, especially as they relate to issues brought up by today's session.

3. <u>Meditate on and memorize Proverbs 12:1.</u> Meditating means repeating the verse over and over and thinking about its meaning and applications.
Write the verse on an index card and put it where you can see it. Work on the verse daily for at least a week.

Encourage students to list prayer needs for others in their books so they can pray for one another during the week. Assign a student coordinator in each small group to gather the group's requests and e-mail them to the group members.

Prayer Connection:

This is the time to encourage, support, and pray for each other in our journeys to grasp the importance of relationships to our spiritual growth.

Share prayer needs with the group, especially those related to finding and connecting with other Christ-followers who will help you to feel loved and accepted while learning more about God's plan for you. Your group facilitator will close your time in prayer.

Prayer Needs:

Encourage students to dig a little deeper by completing a "Now What" assignment before the next time you meet. Remind students about the "Get Ready" short daily Bible readings and related questions at the beginning of session 9.

Show the group you love them. Tell them that you've been praying for them.

 **now What?**

Deepen your understanding of who God is and continue the journey you've begun today by choosing one of the following assignments to complete this week:

Option 1:
Spend time this week listening to what others say to you. Are you often criticized? What are you criticized for the most? Are the criticisms valid? Truly listen and write a paragraph detailing what you learn about yourself this week.

Option 2:
Write a letter to your parents telling them you are thankful for their correction. Share with them a time when they corrected you for which you are now thankful. Explain how you felt when you were first corrected and how you feel now. Tell them you know they corrected you because they really do love you. If you need to apologize for not accepting their correction and discipline, do so.

Bible Reference notes

Use these notes to deepen your understanding as you study the Bible on your own:

Proverbs 13:24

the rod. In this culture the rod was used for spanking. Proverbs consistently reinforces the importance of discipline, regardless of the method of discipline or punishment (10:13; 22:15; 29:15).

Proverbs 15:32

instruction. God's discipline or moral correction is included in His love for us. Hebrews, as well as other New Testament books, repeats that truth (Heb. 12:7-11). We are to heed discipline or regret foolishness (5:11-12).

Proverbs 28:23

Rebukes are welcomed by the wise. But flattery is never effective with the wise and discerning.

Session

9

IF MONEY TALKS . . .
WHAT IS IT SAYING?

Connections Prep

MAIN LIFEPOINT:
Money is a necessity in life; however, if you live your life solely for the pleasure money brings, you will be left feeling empty. Money cannot buy joy or satisfaction. God desires for us to use our money to bless others.

To reinforce the LifePoint, leaders and small-group facilitators should understand the following more detailed CheckPoints and "Do" Points.

BIBLE STUDY CHECKPOINTS:
· Recognize the wisdom in saving money
· Become accountable for our spending habits
· Give according to God's plan

LIFE CHANGE "DO" POINTS:
· Commit to evaluate your purchases before you make them
· Use money in a way that brings glory to God
· Learn to be a joyful giver

PREPARATION:
☐ Review the leader book for this session and prepare your teaching.
☐ Determine how you will subdivide students into small discussion groups.
☐ Recruit mature students or adults as small-group facilitators. Be sure these facilitators plan to attend.
☐ Recruit volunteers or leaders for the "Say What?" activity

REQUIRED SUPPLIES:
☐ *Proverbs: Uncommon Sense* leader books for each group facilitator
☐ *Proverbs: Uncommon Sense* student books for each student
☐ Pens or pencils for each student
☐ Two pennies for each student in attendance

 Get Ready

Read one of these short Bible passages each day and spend a few minutes wrapping your brain around it. Be sure to jot down any insights you discover.

MONDAY   **Read Proverbs 11:24-26.**
How tightly do you hold on to what you have? Do you grudgingly let others borrow your things, or do you freely allow them to use your belongings? Why or why not?

TUESDAY   **Read Proverbs 19:17.**
How does God reward kindness? Will you be more generous now that you know that God repays kindness? How can you be more generous this week?

WEDNESDAY   **Read Proverbs 22:7.**
According to this passage, what is wrong with going into debt for things you really want? How does the Bible portray the person who is in debt to someone else?

THURSDAY   **Read Proverbs 23:4-5.**
Why is it so difficult to get rich? How can someone your age get trapped by greed? How does an obsession with money affect your life?

FRIDAY

Read Proverbs 27:23-27.

According to this passage, what do you need to worry about? How do you manage your money?

SATURDAY

Read Proverbs 28:8.

How would you feel if a close friend offered to assist your family, who was desperately in need of money. How would your feelings change if they charged interest in order to make money on the situation?

SUNDAY

Read Proverbs 28:27.

How do you define "poor"? Why is it so easy to look the other way when you see someone in need? Describe a time when you forced yourself to ignore someone in need.

LARGE-GROUP OPENING:
Get everyone's attention. Make announcements. Open your session with a prayer. Read the LifePoint to the students.

Regarding last week's "Now What?" ask students where they feel like they need the most improvement after having a week to listen and pray about it.

 LifePoint

Money is a necessity in life; however, if you live your life solely for the pleasure money brings, you will be left feeling empty. Money cannot buy joy or satisfaction. God desires for us to use our money to bless others.

SMALL-GROUP TIME:
Instruct students to separate into smaller groups of 4-8, preferably in a circle configuration. Call on the mature student or adult leaders you recruited to facilitate each small group through this "Say What?" segment.

Say What? *(15 MINUTES)*

Random Question of the Week:
Why is the abbreviation for pounds (weight) lbs?

Group Experience: Blinded By Money
Divide your large group into teams of 3 to 5. Give each student two pennies and place a big container—as small as a plastic cup or as big as a cardboard box, depending on how challenging you want to make the game—in the center of the room. Give each team a piece of paper that can be used as a scorecard. Each team must keep the scorecard on hand at all times. Put several leaders around the container in the center of the room to award to points (1 point for each penny) each time a player is successful in dropping the coins into the container.

Instruct players to play the game like this. Each member will take turns tilting his or her head back as a penny is placed over each closed eye. (Contact lens wearers be careful.) It is the objective of this person to follow the verbal commands of the other group members as they direct him or her toward the container in order to drop the penny off the face and into the container.

One point is awarded for each penny successfully dropped into the container. Then return, preferably to a different starting point, and do it again with the next person. The group should alternate turns until time is up.

Give students about five to seven minutes to complete the activity.

After the exercise, ask these follow-up questions:

1. How difficult was it to follow your teammates' voices? Were you able to concentrate on the voices of your team or were you distracted by the money you had on your eyes?

2. Are you a person who is more proud when you buy something expensive or when you get "the deal of a lifetime"? Have you ever purchased something you never used? Why?

3. Have you ever thought you just had to have something, only to find out a few days later it wasn't all you thought it would be? Describe that item and why it fizzled.

LARGE-GROUP TIME:
Have the students turn
to face the front for
this teaching time. Be
sure you can make
eye contact with each
student in the room.
Encourage students to
follow along and take
notes in their student
books.

Share the "So What?"
information with your
large group of students.
You may modify it with
your own perspectives
and teaching needs.
Be sure to highlight the
underlined information,
which gives answers
to the student book
questions and fill-in-
the-blanks (shown in
the margins).

So What? *(30 MINUTES)*

Teaching Outline

I. Heart Treasure
   A. Your values are reflected in your spending
   B. God cares about how we spend, save, and view our money
   C. Money is a window to the human heart

II. Proverbs 11:24-26; 19:17; 22:7; 23:4-5; 27:23-27; 28:8,27

III. The Love of Money
   A. Money itself is not evil
   B. God commends generosity
   C. The more you give, the more God rewards

IV. Pointless Riches
   A. Don't wear yourself out chasing money
   B. Money doesn't provide happiness
   C. Don't make decisions that are motivated by money

V. The Generosity of the Wise
   A. Money is a way to help others
   B. God blesses those who are generous
   C. Now is the time to learn to be wise and generous

VI. The Folly of Debt
   A. The borrower never has the advantage
   B. Credit cards provide instant purchase power and instant debt
   C. It is difficult to help others when you are in debt

VII. The Folly of Selfish Enrichment
   A. Save with a goal in mind
   B. Hoarding money deprives others of help
   C. Do not harm others financially for your own benefit

VIII. The Wisdom of Knowing Your Flocks
   A. Take the time to plan your finances
   B. Create a budget
   C. Live within your budget

9

**TEACHING FOR THE
LARGE GROUP**

Heart Treasure

Your values are reflected in your spending. Some families spend only to survive. Others have barely enough to survive but still find small ways to give to God's work. Some families spend only to enjoy. Others make room for enjoyment and for giving. Some scrimp and save and keep their money all to themselves. Others foolishly give their money away.

God cares about how we spend, save, and view our money. He demands our heart as well as the things we treasure. Because money is a window to the human heart, our treasure and desires are reflected in the items we purchase. This is why Jesus said, "Where your treasure is, there your heart will be also" (Matt. 6:21). Our attitude toward money is a spiritual issue. We can view our money as completely ours, or we can view it as something that is on loan to us from God.

Learning from the Bible

Before the session, enlist a student to read Proverbs 11:24-26; 19:17; 22:7; 23:4-5; 27:23-27; 28:8,27.

One person gives freely, yet gains more;
another withholds what is right, only to become poor.
A generous person will be enriched,
and the one who gives a drink of water will receive water.
People will curse anyone who hoards grain,
but a blessing will come to the one who sells it.—Proverbs 11:24-26

Kindness to the poor is a loan to the LORD,
and He will give a reward to the lender.—Proverbs 19:17

The rich rule over the poor, and the borrower is a slave to the lender.—Proverbs 22:7

Don't wear yourself out to get rich; stop giving your attention to it.
As soon as your eyes fly to it, it disappears,
for it makes wings for itself and flies like an eagle to the sky.—Proverbs 23:4-5

Know well the condition of your flock, and pay attention to your herds,
for wealth is not forever; not even a crown lasts for all time.
When hay is removed and new growth appears
and the grain from the hills is gathered in, lambs will provide your clothing,
and goats, the price of a field;
there will be enough goat's milk for your food—food for your household
and nourishment for your servants.—Proverbs 27:23-27

LARGE-GROUP TIME
CONTINUED:
This is the meat of the
teaching time. Remind
students to follow along
and take notes in their
student books.

As you share the
"So What?" information
with students, make
it your own. Use your
natural teaching style.

Emphasize underlined
information, which gives
answers to the student
book questions or fill-in-
the-blanks in the (shown
in the margins).

❶ According to
1 Timothy 6:10, what is
root of all evil?

❷ How is God's view of
money balanced?

❸ How will God's
philosophy of money
benefit you?

❹ Why is not worth
it to wear yourself out
getting rich?

Whoever increases his wealth through excessive interest
collects it for one who is kind to the poor.—Proverbs 28:8

The one who gives to the poor will not be in need,
but one who turns his eyes away will receive many curses.—Proverbs 28:27

The Love of Money

Many people misquote 1 Timothy 6:10 ❶ to mean, "Money is the root of all evil." The verse actually says, "The love of money is a root of all kinds of evil." In other words, there is nothing evil about money itself. Loving money is what leads to various kinds of evil.

❷ God's view of money is not communistic (everybody shares equally) or imperialist (everyone builds their own empire). God does not condemn saving money for future security; He commends it. Also, God does not condone hoarding wealth; He commends generosity. Adopting God's philosophy of money will save you a lot of pain and anxiety. ❸ If you submit your finances to God, you will not be in need, and you will be able to help others. You will be a person who "gives freely, yet gains more" (Prov. 11:24).

As a teenager you may have money that you have worked hard for, you may have no money available, or you may receive an allowance from your parents. You might have a parent who willingly gives you whatever you want, or you might have a parent who requires you to save and prioritize your spending. Regardless of where your money comes from, it is important to understand that what you spend your money on and what your motives are for spending reveal what is truly important to you.

Pointless Riches

Many of us dream of being rich, but this dream is not worth our time and effort. Solomon advises, "Don't wear yourself out to get rich" (Prov. 23:4). ❹ There are things in life worth wearing ourselves out for, but wealth is not one of them. Only a small number of people become wealthy. When they do become wealthy, there is usually a great amount of risk, effort, and worry involved. As a result, they are usually not as happy as they imagined they would be once they achieve their goal. Wealth is elusive. Solomon says it "makes wings for itself and flies like an eagle" (Prov. 23:5). One reason for this is competition. Because so many people want to be wealthy, the competition is fierce and unfriendly.

Getting rich should not be your life's goal. It is hard for many people to believe this, but the sooner you learn this truth, the better your balance of life, family, and money will be. Don't allow money to decide your occupation or where you go to school. These decisions should not be motivated by money. Our culture today encourages us to succeed, become famous, and spend lavishly. However, when we only look out for ourselves, we overlook people in need.

The Generosity of the Wise

While some people wear themselves out trying to get rich, others focus on money as a way to help themselves and others. Ironically, some of the most generous people always seem to have enough (Prov. 11:24). Instead of holding on to money, generous people like to use it to bless others. ❺ Consequently, God rewards them. They often have true friends, a loving family, and great happiness.

❺ Why do generous people usually have plenty?

❻ The key difference between the tight-fisted individual and the joyful giver is humility. The giver sees others as more important than himself. He is not interested in hoarding. He supports God's work and gives his money wisely to people in need. When he helps someone, he does not miss the money. He sees his giving as a loan that God will repay (Prov. 19:17). He builds treasure in heaven rather than on earth. And usually, he finds himself well-supplied (Prov. 28:27).

❻ What is the key difference between a hoarder and a giver?

The average family in Haiti lives on a little more than $300 per year. Many teenagers spend that much on music downloads in a year but are unwilling to give to organizations and ministries that help people in need. Others choose to do without something as simple as a cup of coffee so that they will have money to give to those in need. The perfect time for you to learn to be wise and generous with your money is now.

The Folly of Debt

If you want to be wise and generous with your money, you must be in a position where you can be generous. Nothing drains resources like debt does. A borrower is in many ways a slave to the lender (Prov. 22:7). If a creditor wants to raise the interest rate or call the loan, the borrower has no choice in the matter. A borrower can never get ahead because he is behind.

Countless students enter college financially inexperienced. They are used to new clothes, cell phones, and computers, and they quickly get into debt to maintain that lifestyle. Many soon discover that repaying their debts is next to impossible. They wind up missing classes and even putting their educations on hold in order to work and repay their debts. ❼ The Bible does not forbid borrowing, but it warns against the folly of it. Borrowing can be wise, especially if the debt is secured. A

❼ Does the Bible forbid borrowing money? Why or why not?

car loan or home mortgage is an example of secured debt. It's considered secured because the car or the home can be sold in order for the debt to be repaid. However, unsecured debt (like credit card debt) is very dangerous. It is considered high-risk because it provides benefit today but risk tomorrow. Jobs can be lost. Disasters can happen. Everything can vanish very quickly, especially when there is unsecured debt involved. It is hard to help yourself or others when you are in debt.

When you obsess over the best clothes or the nicest car, your priorities need a check. What is wrong with the clothes you have? What keeps you from wanting to drive an older car? We live in a culture that teaches us our wants are more important than anything else. We must guard ourselves from falling in love with money—which is the root of all evil (1 Tim. 6:10).

The Folly of Selfish Enrichment

If it is foolish to borrow unsecured money, it is just as foolish to hoard wealth. Saving is different from hoarding. You save with a goal in mind. For instance, you save a reserve in case of a job loss or a fund for an education. You save for travel or gifts. ❽ Hoarding occurs when you withhold giving when you can afford to help (Prov. 11:24).

❽ **What is the definition of hoarding?**

It is also foolish to enrich yourself by harming others (Prov. 28:8). If you choose to oppress others, God will judge you. Whether you ask your friends for unnecessary gas money or order the most expensive item on the menu because someone else is paying, God always sees your motives and knows your heart.

The Wisdom of Knowing Your Flocks

To become wise with your money, put these principles to work. Gain a balanced view of wealth and generosity. Save, invest, and give to others. Many students expect to wake up one morning financially wise. They live their lives spending other people's money, and they don't worry about where the money comes from. Then, they find themselves in trouble financially when they are on their own.

One of the most important ways to become financially wise is to know your flock (Prov. 27:23). The owner of sheep is a businessman. He knows which sheep will breed well and which ones will not. He knows when an animal needs to be sold or kept. He knows how to keep his sheep safe. ❾ In order for you to know your financial "flock", you must live within a budget. Do not spend more than you make, regardless of what you want or what someone else has. A sheep rancher doesn't leave things to chance. He estimates and prepares for his needs. He knows the present and saves for the future. He knows that wealth is not forever (Prov. 27:24).

❾ **What steps can you take to know your "flock"?**

SMALL-GROUP TIME:
Use this time to help students begin to integrate the truth they've learned into their lives while they connect with other students in the group, the leaders, and with God.

After presenting the teaching material, ask students to divide back into small groups and discuss the "Do What?" questions. Small group facilitators should lead the discussions and set they tone by being open and honest in responding to each question.

Do What? *(15 MINUTES)*

1. Tell a story about the most foolish purchase you ever made. Why did you make it? Where is that item now?

2. How do you rate on the financial wisdom scale? Check one.
   - ☐ Money disappears in my wallet.
   - ☐ I'm so tight! I bring a calculator to calculate tips to the exact penny.
   - ☐ I spend money so fast that I look like a card dealer at a casino.
   - ☐ I give money away because it helps me get friends.
   - ☐ I am looking forward to getting my first credit card. I already know what I'm going to buy with it.
   - ☐ Other: _____

3. Do you believe God really cares about how you spend your money? What is something someone has done with their money that has really impressed you? Have you ever known someone who gives away money but always seems to have more?

4. Why do you think the Bible says God loves a "cheerful giver" (2 Cor. 9:7)? How would you describe a cheerful giver? What motivates a cheerful giver to give?

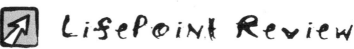

LifePoint Review

Money is a necessity in life; however, if you live your life solely for the pleasure money brings, you will be left feeling empty. Money can not buy joy or satisfaction. God desires for us to use our money to bless others.

"Do" Points:

These "Do" Points will help you grab hold of this week's LifePoint. Be open and honest as you answer the questions within your small group.

1. <u>Commit to evaluate your purchases before you make them.</u> Are you guilty of buying things you don't need but want? Do you have a closet full of things you wanted last year but wouldn't be caught dead in this year? **How will you seek God's wisdom concerning your purchases?**

2. <u>Use money in a way that brings glory to God.</u> When we use money for God's glory to further His Kingdom, God is pleased. When we spend money without considering how it will affect our ability to give to God, we are not being financially wise. **How do you currently spend money? How can you become a better money manager?**

3. <u>Learn to be a joyful giver.</u> What is your attitude like when you give money to others? Do you resent giving what you have worked so hard for? Do you look for the money to come back to you? Do you feel like you're better than other people are because you gave (Mark 12:41-44)? **What is one thing you can do this week to be a joyful giver?**

Prayer Connection:

This is the time to encourage, support, and pray for each other in our journeys to trust God and seek out real and personal encounters with Him.

Share prayer needs with the group, especially those related to hearing from and responding to God. Your group facilitator will close your time in prayer.

Prayer Needs:

now What?

Deepen your understanding of who God is, and continue the journey you've begun today by choosing one of the following assignments to complete this week:

Option 1:
Make a point to keep a budget this week. Yes, it's true, budgets are not very exciting or adventurous, but a budget is a great way to understand habits and tendencies. During the week, keep track of every penny you spend. This is a tedious assignment, but very doable for a week. At the end of the week take a look at everything you spent and what it bought. Are you happy with your decisions? Are there instances that you wish you could "do over"? Be prepared to talk about your findings next week.

Option 2:
Find a worthy cause to donate money to this week. Do without something you want, or work some odd jobs for the extra funds. Look for a way to be wise in your generosity as you give without expecting anything in return. Journal honestly about your thoughts and feelings as you go through this process. Be prepared to share your thoughts at next week's meeting.

Bible Reference notes

Use these notes to deepen your understanding as you study the Bible on your own:

Proverbs 11:24 — ***gives freely, yet gains.*** This is a paradox. Generosity, not hoarding, is the path to prosperity.

Proverbs 22:7 — ***slave.*** Often in ancient culture people had to enslave themselves to pay off debts. The slave here refers to anyone in debt.

Proverbs 27:23-27 — This passage celebrates the security and the cycle of an agricultural society.

Encourage students to dig a little deeper by completing a "Now What?" assignment before the next time you meet. Remind students about the "Get Ready" short daily Bible readings and related questions at the beginning session 10.

Ask about specific prayer requests from the week before. Tell them that you're praying for them!

Session

10

THE LORD AND WISDOM

Connections Prep

MAIN LIFEPOINT:
The road to wisdom ultimately leads to God. We become wise when we realize that God sees all, knows all, and influences everything that happens in this world. He punishes evil and favors righteousness. Wisdom is the Lord's, and those with wisdom fear Him.

To reinforce the LifePoint, leaders and small-group facilitators should understand the following more detailed CheckPoints and "Do" Points.

BIBLE STUDY CHECKPOINTS:
- Understand that God has total knowledge of and influence over all of creation
- Believe in God's justice and love for His followers
- Seek a growing relationship with God and gain wisdom through Him

LIFE CHANGE "DO" POINTS:
- Commit to understand that God sees EVERY part of your life
- Eliminate areas of your life that distract you from God
- Learn to accept the plans that God has for you

PREPARATION:
- ☐ Review the leader book for this session and prepare your teaching.
- ☐ Determine how you will subdivide students into small discussion groups.
- ☐ Recruit mature students or adults as small-group facilitators. Be sure these facilitators plan to attend.

REQUIRED SUPPLIES:
- ☐ *Proverbs: Uncommon* leader books for each group facilitator
- ☐ *Proverbs: Uncommon* student books for each student
- ☐ Pens or pencils for each student
- ☐ One bag of cookies for each small group
- ☐ One plate/serving tray for each small group

10

 Get Ready

Read one of these short Bible passages each day and spend a few minutes wrapping your brain around it. Be sure to jot down any insights you discover.

MONDAY

Read Proverbs 10:29; 18:10.
Is God your strong tower? Why? What has He done to deserve that title?

TUESDAY

Read Proverbs 15:11; 20:27.
How much does God really know about you? Describe something you have done when you forgot God was there.

WEDNESDAY

Read Proverbs 16:9; 20:24.
How does God plan your steps? Can we choose to take a different path than the one God has laid before us? How could you have avoided some problems by following the steps God laid out for you?

THURSDAY

Read Proverbs 16:33; 19:21.
What is something unexpected God has done for you? How do you know it was God? Have you ever used God as an excuse to do something you wanted to do, so others wouldn't question your motives?

FRIDAY

Read Proverbs 15:29; 16:5.

Do you think that what you do helps or hinders your prayers? Why?

SATURDAY

Read Proverbs 19:23.

Describe a time when God protected you from evil. How did you feel about His protection at the time? How do you feel about it now?

SUNDAY

Read Proverbs 29:25.

Why do we sometimes worry more about pleasing others than about pleasing God? Describe a time in your life when you tried to please someone other than God. What was the outcome?

LARGE-GROUP OPENING:
Get everyone's attention. Make announcements. Open your session with a prayer. Read the LifePoint to the students.

Ask the group if anyone chose Option 1 from last week's "Now What?" Allow volunteers to share what they learned during the exercise.

 LifePoint

10

The road to wisdom ultimately leads to God. We become wise when we realize that God sees all, knows all, and influences everything that happens in this world. He punishes evil and favors righteousness. Wisdom is the Lord's, and those with wisdom fear Him.

SMALL-GROUP TIME:
Instruct students to separate into smaller groups of 4-8, preferably in a circle configuration. Call on the mature student or adult leaders you recruited to facilitate each small group through this "Say What?" segment.

Say What? *(15 MINUTES)*

Random Question of the Week:
Who is the funniest cartoon character?

Group Experience: Cookie Tower

Open the bag of cookies and distribute the cookies to the students. Give each student an equal number of cookies. Tell students to build one tower for their group by placing their cookies on the plate/serving tray one at a time. Have students alternate placing the cookies on the tower so that everyone has a chance to participate. After the tower falls, give students a chance to build another. See how many "cookies high" they can build their tower. If the students find this task too easy, suggest they try to stack the cookies without using their hands.

After the exercise, ask these follow-up questions:

1. How difficult was it to see your tower fall? How did it feel to watch your tower fall because someone else wrongly placed a cookie? Were you disappointed to see something you created crumble before your eyes?

2. What is the one thing you are the most proud of "creating" in your life? What makes that thing so special? Did you take your time and put extra energy into creating it? Why?

3. What is the one thing you have created that has brought you the most disappointment? Did you have a vision of something beautiful in your head, but the finished project didn't come out that way? Describe what you created and how it looked when you were finished.

 **So What?** *(30 MINUTES)*

LARGE-GROUP TIME:
Have the students turn
to face the front for
this teaching time. Be
sure you can make eye
contact with each student
in the room. Encourage
students to follow along
and take notes in their
student books.

Teaching Outline

I. Wisdom in His Word
    A. God knows how things need to work and how they should look
    B. He shares His wisdom with us in the Bible

II. Proverbs 10:29; 15:11,29; 16:5,9,33; 18:10; 19:21,23; 20:24,27; 29:25

III. God's Wisdom
    A. God is the central figure in Solomon's wisdom proverbs
    B. God created the world with wisdom
    C. Without God, the world's wisdom doesn't make sense

IV. God in Our Hearts and Minds
    A. Mysteries to us are not mysteries to God
    B. God sees into our thoughts and emotions

V. God Behind the Scenes
    A. God is behind the details of our lives
    B. Only God knows our future

VI. God Directs the Madness
    A. Life is not controlled by random chance
    B. God is ultimately in control
    C. God doesn't get surprised

VII. God's Favor and Justice
    A. We sometimes doubt God's justice
    B. Pride and apathy are two common religious sins
    C. God hears the prayers of the righteous

VIII. Pleasing God
    A. We often fear consequences from people, whom we can see, more than the displeasure of God, whom we can't see
    B. God should direct us, not people

10

IX. Under His Protection
A. The Old Testament—Tower
B. The protection given by God

TEACHING FOR THE LARGE GROUP:
Share the "So What?" teaching with your students. You may modify it to fit your needs.

Be sure to highlight the underlined information, which gives answers to the student book questions and fill-in-the-blanks (shown in the margins).

Before the session, enlist a student to read Proverbs 10:29; 15:11,29; 16:5,9,33; 18:10; 19:21,23; 20:24,27; 29:25.

Wisdom in His Word

We have all taken the time and energy to create something. Whether it was a paper plate decorated like a turkey for Thanksgiving in kindergarten or a finger painting of a Christmas tree, we have all made something for someone. Probably we have also created something that didn't quite come out the way we originally planned. God, however, has never had that problem. When He created the world, He was successful from the beginning. He shares this wisdom with us in His Word.

Learning from the Bible

The way of the LORD is a stronghold for the honorable,
but destruction awaits the malicious.–Proverbs 10:29

Sheol and Abaddon lie open before the LORD—
how much more, human hearts.–Proverbs 15:11

The LORD is far from the wicked,
but He hears the prayer of the righteous.–Proverbs 15:29

Everyone with a proud heart is detestable to the LORD;
be assured, he will not go unpunished.–Proverbs 16:5

A man's heart plans his way,
but the LORD determines his steps.–Proverbs 16:9

The lot is cast into the lap,
but its every decision is from the LORD.–Proverbs 16:33

The name of the LORD is a strong tower;
the righteous run to it and are protected.–Proverbs 18:10

Many plans are in a man's heart,
but the LORD's decree will prevail.–Proverbs 19:21

LARGE-GROUP TIME CONTINUED:
This is the meat of the teaching time. Remind students to follow along and take notes in their student books.

As you share the "So What?" information with students, make it your own. Use your natural teaching style.

Emphasize underlined information, which gives answers to the student book questions or fill-in-the-blanks in the (shown in the margins).

The fear of the Lord leads to life;
one will sleep at night without danger.–Proverbs 19:23

A man's steps are determined by the Lord,
so how can anyone understand his own way.–Proverbs 20:24

A person's breath is the lamp of the Lord,
searching the innermost parts.–Proverbs 20:27

The fear of man is a snare,
but the one who trusts in the Lord is protected.–Proverbs 29:25

God's Wisdom

It is evident that wisdom and God are bound together. In the first nine chapters of Proverbs, Solomon makes God the central figure. He says that fearing God is the beginning, or foundation, of wisdom (Prov. 1:7). We are to trust in the Lord with all our heart and not rely on our own understanding (Prov. 3:5). We are told that God made wisdom as the first of all His works (Prov. 8:22). ❶ To say that wisdom is God's creation is a graceful way to say that God made the world run according to wisdom. Therefore, God can tell us what to expect when we deal with people because God made people. He understands our nature. The world is not a mystery to God. He understands the depths of His creation.

❶ How is wisdom the creation of God?

There are forces pulling against us that would have us believe that we do not need God's wisdom. The sort of "wisdom" we get apart from God is "iffy" at best. And where would this "wisdom" come from? It might come from some so-called expert on television, a celebrity or movie star, or maybe a professional athlete. These types are not lacking for air time, for sure, so their "wisdom" almost always finds its channel. ❷ But wisdom apart from God lacks substance. It lacks truth and value. Much of the time it has absolutely no basis, rather it's just somebody's opinion, while other times these revelations only tell part of the story—the other part comes from what the speaker wants to happen. Godly wisdom is pure, with no agenda other than His love for you and me.

❷ How does the world's wisdom lack truth and value?

10

God in Our Hearts and Minds

Countless mysteries exist that are beyond even the greatest thinkers' and problem solvers' abilities to explain. People spend years of their lives trying to understand things that only God can comprehend. They dream of figuring God out one day, but they never will because God is so much greater (Isa. 55:8-9). He understands things that are mysterious to us. He sees right into our thoughts and emotions (Prov. 15:11).

Our spirit is another mysterious place inside of us. The Hebrews used the same word for *spirit* and *breath*. This may be because when we die, we lose our breath. ❸ Breath is at least a fitting symbol for the spirit. To God, our spirit is like a lamp shining inside us (Prov. 20:27). God reads our spirits as easily as we can see a person's face. None of our thoughts or emotions are hidden from Him. Nothing is closed to God, not even our deepest thoughts and desires.

❸ Explain the significance between the Hebrew words for "spirit" and "breath." How is our spirit like our breath?

God Behind the Scenes

Life does not always go as planned. Sometimes the smartest or strongest don't win. There are times when a promising young person dies, a foolproof plan fails, or an expectation disappoints. There are also times when the underdog wins. We need to remember that there is an unseen player in the details of life. People may plan, but God is behind the scenes. Only He knows all the details and influences affecting events in our lives.

❹ Why can't we predict how things will turn out?

Not only does God know the details, He also influences the outcomes. The Bible teaches that God influences what happens. ❹ Though men may plan, God decides what happens (Prov. 16:9). We may think we control the future, but God plans the steps. Therefore, we cannot know the way before us with certainty (Prov. 20:24). Only God is wise.

God Directs the Madness

God did not choose for us the madness that we experience in life. We chose it. Yet, God re-directs the madness and moves it in the direction He desires. Life seems random at times, like a roll of the dice, but we know that's not the case. Solomon says that God even decides the outcome of the casting of lots (Prov. 16:33).

❺ Why won't we ever be successful at controlling life?

Even when we plot and scheme, we cannot control life. It is not random or able to be controlled. ❺ Life is ultimately under God's influence and control (Prov. 19:21), and we must accept that when we don't understand why things happen the way they do, God does. He is never surprised or caught off guard.

God's Favor and Justice

❻ Why do people doubt God's justice?

❻ Bad guys seem to get away with evil, and good guys seem to lose frequently in the struggle for Christian values. As a result, we sometimes doubt God's justice. Because of His grace, God created us with the ability to follow Him and love Him because we choose to, not because we have to. If He did not give us a choice, what would we be? We would be nothing but robots following orders from a controller rather than a loving Creator.

Pride and apathy (a lack of concern) are two very common religious sins. God does not reward pride; in fact, He will punish it in the end (Prov. 16:5). Nor should we fail to be concerned about goodness and character because we think God is already on our side. ❼ <u>God hears the prayers of the righteous (Prov. 15:29). Though we know our acceptance by Him is not based on good deeds, He nonetheless favors obedience as any father who wants to reward his obedient children.</u> God's favor and justice are real, even if we don't always think they're evident (Matt. 7:9-11).

❼ How does our obedience or disobedience affect how God answers prayer?

Pleasing God

Recognizing that God sees all, knows all, and influences all should cause us to have a healthy fear (a respectful reverence because of His holiness and perfection) of Him. Yet, foolishly, we often fear consequences from people, whom we can see, more than the displeasure of God (Prov. 29:25), whom we can't see. Yet, it is God who should direct us, not people. When we strive for approval from our friends and peers, we put our faith in people instead of in Christ. A wise person concerns himself with pleasing God, not people.

Under His Protection

❽ <u>In the ancient world, many people worked in the fields. When a raiding army would come, these workers would run into the walls of the nearby town. Some towns had towers as well as walls. The tower was the ultimate defense for a town because it gave the advantage of height to defeat besieging armies.</u> ❾ <u>Having a relationship with God is like having a tower for protection (Prov. 18:10). Trouble may come, but the tower will prevail.</u> Peace is the reward of knowing the God who sees and knows everything (Prov. 29:25). God is a stronghold for those who follow His ways (Prov. 10:29). The wise person trusts in the Lord rather than leaning on what he sees and hears, for God sees and hears more than we can ever know.

❽ How did a tower provide protection in ancient societies?

❾ Compare your relationship with God to a strong tower.

SMALL-GROUP TIME: Use this time to help students begin to integrate the truth they've learned into their lives while they connect with other students in the group, the leaders, and with God.

 Do What? *(15 MINUTES)*

10

1. How is God in charge of your life? What part of your life do you struggle giving to God?

After presenting the teaching material, ask students to divide back into small groups and discuss the "Do What?" questions. Small group facilitators should lead the discussions and set they tone by being open and honest in responding to each question.

2. How big a part does God play in your daily life? Check one.

☐ I don't think about God during my daily life.

☐ I feel God's presence when I am in church or small group.

☐ I sense God in the quiet everyday moments.

☐ I know God is there, but I'm not aware of Him most of the time.

☐ Sometimes I sense God throughout the day, and other times I tend to forget Him.

☐ God is always there, though I sometimes choose to ignore Him.

☐ Other: _____

3. Do you believe God knows everything? How does that affect your life?

4. Do your friends think about God regularly? When was the last time you had a conversation about God with a friend? Where were you? Why did your conversation involve God?

Small-group facilitators should reinforce the LifePoint for this session. Make sure that student's questions are invited and addressed honestly.

 # LifePoint Review

The road to wisdom ultimately leads to God. We become wise when we realize that God sees all, knows all, and influences everything that happens in this world. He punishes evil and favors righteousness. Wisdom is the Lord's, and those with wisdom fear Him.

Do" Points:

These "Do" Points will help you grab hold of this week's LifePoint. Be open and honest as you answer the questions within your small group.

1. <u>Commit to understand that God sees EVERY part of your life.</u> According to Psalm 139, we cannot get away from God and His presence. No matter where we go, God is there. When we understand that God created everything, we have nowhere to hide.
   How often do you find yourself embarrassed by your choices when you realize that God is aware of what you are doing?

2. <u>Eliminate areas of your life that distract you from God.</u> What would happen if you chose to stay away from a certain activity, event, place, or group of people? Would you be able to focus more on God?
   Name two things in your life that are keeping you from God. How could you eliminate these distractions?

3. <u>Learn to accept the plans that God has for you.</u> How do you feel when random events happen to you? What is your first reaction? Do you view the unexpected events in your life as coincidence or an opportunity from God?
   How can you release control of your life to God?

Prayer Connection:

This is the time to encourage, support, and pray for each other in our journeys to trust God and seek out real and personal encounters with Him.

Share prayer needs with the group, especially those related to hearing from and responding to God. Your group facilitator will close your time in prayer.

Prayer Needs:

Be sure to end your session by asking students to share prayer needs with one another, especially as they relate to issues brought up by today's session.

Encourage students to list prayer needs for others in their books so they can pray for one another during the week. Assign a student coordinator in each small group to gather the group's requests and e-mail them to the group members.

10

Encourage students to dig a little deeper by completing a "Now What?" assignment before the next time you meet. Remind students about the "Get Ready" short daily Bible readings and related questions at the beginning of the next session.

now What?

Deepen your understanding of who God is and continue the journey you've begun today by choosing one of the following assignments to complete this week:

Option 1:
God is all-knowing. It is true that He sees everything at once. As you go about your week, be very aware that the Holy Spirit is present. When watching television or talking with friends or even while you're out running errands, how different would it be if Jesus was physically alongside. How would it change your thoughts or how you perceive certain things? Come prepared next week to mention one instance and how His presence would have changed the circumstances.

Option 2:
Make a list of truths that you know because of God's Word. You might list items like "I know God created the earth" or "God is love." Think about the things on your list and imagine how your life would be different if you did not know these facts to be true. Pray for God to show you how necessary the Bible and faith are to gaining wisdom. Bring your list next week and be prepared to share it with those in your small group.

Bible Reference Notes

Use these notes to deepen your understanding as you study the Bible on your own:

Proverbs 15:11   ***Sheol and Abaddon.*** This is probably an allusion to the fact that God sees the dead in their graves or in their eternal homes. How much more should God be able to see the hearts of living people?

Proverbs 16:9   ***plans his way.*** God's sovereignty over our lives should not discourage us from planning and setting goals. However, we need God's wisdom to guide us.

Proverbs 20:27   ***searching the innermost parts.*** King David asked God to search him out (Ps. 139:23). (See also Hebrews 4:12 for another way of being "found" by God.)

10

NOTES

Session

11

INTO FOCUS

Connections Prep

MAIN LIFEPOINT: Everyone can use a little more self-control and hard work in their lives. Laziness leads to boredom. God advises us to have self-control and work hard in life.

To reinforce the LifePoint, leaders and small-group facilitators should understand the following more detailed CheckPoints and "Do" Points.

BIBLE STUDY CHECKPOINTS:
- Believe in the wisdom of hard work and self-control
- Understand the principles of hard work
- Recognize the importance of a life plan of self-control and hard work

LIFE CHANGE "DO" POINTS:
- Commit to work hard in all you do
- Search your life for distracting addictions
- Recognize laziness in your life

PREPARATION:
- ☐ Review the leader book for this session and prepare your teaching.
- ☐ Determine how you will subdivide students into small discussion groups.
- ☐ Recruit mature students or adults as small-group facilitators. Be sure these facilitators plan to attend.

REQUIRED SUPPLIES:
- ☐ *Proverbs: Uncommon Sense* leader books for each group facilitator
- ☐ *Proverbs: Uncommon Sense* student books for each student
- ☐ Pens or pencils for each student
- ☐ Bananas and butter knives for every two people
- ☐ Safety pins, sewing needles, tape, and a set of markers for each small group

Get Ready

*Read one of these short Bible passages each day and spend a few minutes
wrapping your brain around it. Be sure to jot down any insights you discover.*

MONDAY

Read Proverbs 10:4 and 12:24.

At what do you work hard? Why? What are the rewards of your hard work? Is it
possible for you to work hard at something that is not worthwhile? Why or why not?

TUESDAY

Read Proverbs 13:4 and 14:23.

Do you know someone who works hard at school? What are the results of his or her
hard work? Do you know someone who wastes his or her time and talents regarding
school? What are the results?

WEDNESDAY

Read Proverbs 10:5.

What is procrastination? When are you most guilty of procrastination? Have you ever
suffered because of it? Why do you choose to procrastinate?

THURSDAY

Read Proverbs 14:4.

Do you ever think school is useless? Why? What things interest you enough to keep
you involved? How could your attitude be better about school?

FRIDAY

Read Proverbs 24:27.

Why do you think setting priorities is important? What are the priorities in your life?

SATURDAY

Read Proverbs 12:27.

Do you take care of your belongings? Why or why not? Have you ever lost something that was important to you? What was your reaction? Could you have avoided losing it by taking better care of it?

SUNDAY

Read Proverbs 20:1 and 23:20-21.

How difficult is it for you to be self-controlled? Who do you know that has the most self-control? Who do you know without any self-control? Who is happier?

LARGE-GROUP OPENING:
Get everyone's attention. Make announcements. Open your session with a prayer. Read the LifePoint to the students.

Ask for any insights from last week's "Now What?"

 LifePoint

Everyone can use a little more self-control and hard work in their lives. Laziness leads to boredom. God advises us to have self-control and work hard in life.

SMALL-GROUP TIME:
Instruct students to
separate into smaller
groups of 4-8,
preferably in a circle
configuration. Call on
the mature student
or adult leaders you
recruited to facilitate
each small group
through this "Say
What?" segment.

 # Say What? *(15 MINUTES)*

Random Question of the Week:
How much time will an average American spend at traffic lights during his or her lifetime?

Group Experience: Banana Surgery

Play a game of "Banana Surgery." Give one banana to every pair of students. Have the pairs decorate their banana with markers and then peel and cut up their banana into equal parts. (Don't tell them what comes next until they're done.) Encourage them to be creative in their decorating and in their surgery. When they are finished with their surgery, tell them they must put the banana back together using pins, needles, tape, and so on.

After the exercise, ask these follow-up questions:

1. Which was more fun, cutting the banana up or trying to put it back together? Why? What made putting the banana back together difficult?

2. If you would have known you had to put the banana back together, would you have done anything differently?

3. Did you feel like putting the banana back together was just too hard? Did you feel tempted to quit, or were you determined to make things work?

LARGE-GROUP TIME:
Have the students turn to face the front for this teaching time. Be sure you can make eye contact with each student in the room. Encourage students to follow along and take notes in their student books.

 # So What? *(30 MINUTES)*

Teaching Outline

I. God's Design
   A. Work was Instituted by God
   B. Our culture that tries to convince us we have truly succeeded when we don't have to work

II. Proverbs 10:4,5; 12:24,27; 13:4; 14:4,23; 20:1; 23:20-21; 24:27

III. God Honors Hard Work
   A. Work in and of itself is not a curse
   B. God rewards hard work
   C. Jesus worked hard on earth

IV. Work to Help Yourself and Others
   A. Hard work and effort are positively recognized
   B. Laziness is negatively recognized

V. Work with a Purpose
   A. Purpose brings value to work
   B. Hard work brings blessings for the future
   C. Extra effort pays off

TEACHING FOR THE LARGE GROUP:
Share the "So What?" teaching with your students. You may modify it to fit your needs.

Be sure to highlight the underlined information, which gives answers to the student book questions and fill-in-the-blanks (shown in the margins).

VI. Work with a Plan
   A. Plan before you begin
   B. Prepare properly for projects

VII. A Hard-Work Attitude
   A. A lazy person doesn't put any effort into his work
   B. A hard worker takes pride in his possessions
   C. A lazy attitude is an enemy

VIII. Distracting Addictions
   A. Addictions distract you from your purpose
   B. Addictions come in various forms

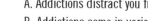

God's Design

Work has existed since the creation of the earth, yet we live in a culture that tries to convince us we have truly succeeded when we don't have to work. Students don't do homework because they think it is unnecessary or because they don't care. ❶ Even before Adam's and Eve's rebellion, God already had work in His plan: "The LORD God took the man and placed him in the garden of Eden to work it and watch over it" (Gen. 2:15). What a job it would have been to tend and shape the direction of God's creation! Though the work would not have had the frustrations of modern gardening, it still would have taken toil and sweat. Work is difficult, but necessary for us.

❶ How did work figure into God's plan for humanity?

Before the session, enlist a student to read Proverbs 10:4,5; 12:24,27; 13:4; 14:4,23; 20:1; 23:20-21; 24:27.

Learning from the Bible

Idle hands make one poor,
but diligent hands bring riches.—Proverbs 10:4

The son who gathers during summer is prudent;
the son who sleeps during harvest is disgraceful.—Proverbs 10:5

The diligent hand will rule,
but laziness will lead to forced labor.—Proverbs 12:24

A lazy man doesn't roast his game,
but to a diligent man, his wealth is precious.—Proverbs 12:27

The slacker craves, yet has nothing,
but the diligent is fully satisfied.—Proverbs 13:4

Where there are no oxen, the feeding-trough is empty,
but an abundant harvest comes through the strength of an ox.—Proverbs 14:4

There is profit in all hard work,
but endless talk leads only to poverty.—Proverbs 14:23

Wine is a mocker, beer is a brawler,
and whoever staggers because of them is not wise.—Proverbs 20:1

❷ Is work part of God's curse on this world? Explain.

❸ What examples are given of God honoring hard and skillful work?

Don't associate with those who drink too much wine,
or with those who gorge themselves on meat.
For the drunkard and the glutton will become poor,
and grogginess will clothe them in rags.–Proverbs 23:20-21

Complete your outdoor work, and prepare your field;
afterwards, build your house.–Proverbs 24:27

God Honors Hard Work

❷ <u>Work itself is not the curse that resulted from the fall of Adam and Eve. Rather, the curse is that working will be difficult, and the land will frustrate man's attempts to put food on the table. Work in and of itself is not a curse.</u>

Solomon gives this description of the lazy life in Proverbs 24:30-34: I went by the field of a slacker and by the vineyard of a man lacking sense. Thistles had come up everywhere, weeds covered the ground, and the stone wall was ruined. I saw and took it to heart; I looked and received instruction: a little sleep, a little slumber, a little folding of the arms to rest, and your poverty will come like a robber, your need like a bandit.

If we were to rewrite his description for teenagers today, it might say: I went to the room of a slacker, and the dirty dishes were hidden under his bed. The hamster cage smelled like it needed to be cleaned and his bed wasn't even visible. His floor was there, but it was covered with clothes, shoes, and "stuff." The only thing in place was his backpack and school books; they looked brand new and unused.

God has always honored good and skillful work. ❸ <u>Skillful men led by Bezalel did the fine work on the curtains and furniture for God's tabernacle. Moses told the people, "The LORD has given them wisdom and understanding to know how to do all the work of constructing the sanctuary" (Ex. 36:1).</u> Notice that wisdom and skilled work are related in this verse. ❸ <u>And when God Himself became a man in the form of Jesus, He was not a loafer. He grew up learning His father's trade of carpentry and woodwork (Mark 6:3).</u> Hard work and self-control are Godly attributes. Our life's mission is to live with a healthy respect and fear of God. This mission ought to spur us toward diligence and self-control in everything we do.

Work to Help Yourself and Others

Solomon's picture of the lazy life is an extreme view, but it's not too far off the mark. Laziness means not taking work seriously because of a lack of purpose. Laziness opposes the very nature of humankind, for we were made to work in the Garden of Eden. After Adam and Eve chose to disobey God, work became full of frustrations. Yet, even in an imperfect world filled with traps, dead ends, and disappointments, our true glory can shine through our work. A parent puts a little creativity into an otherwise ordinary family mealtime. A teacher takes the extra time to listen to her students and treat them with respect. A computer programmer makes the most of his workday by getting done in eight hours what others do in 10. A student works hard to get his homework done so he can help his parents get dinner ready. These are all examples of how work can be used to help ourselves and others.

The Apostle Paul mentioned the importance of work and warned the Thessalonians to avoid the idle person (2 Thess. 3:6-10). Everybody knows that "idle hands make one poor," but it is easy to forget (Prov. 10:4). We can become skeptical and think that no one notices our extra effort or efficiency when we work—even on routine chores around the house. ❹ But most of the time our work is noticed if we do it honestly and well. Eventually, hard-working people exceed the less motivated (Prov. 12:24). By contrast, those who cut corners, make excuses, or waste time generally get noticed, too, in a negative way. They earn their bad grades, don't get special favors, and don't have the respect of their peers. Such slackers generally complain that their lot is not fair. They want respect, promotion, and good grades but never receive them (Prov. 13:4). They often spend time talking instead of working (Prov. 14:23). Eventually the student who works hard and talks less benefits from his hard work, while the lazy student is left behind.

❹ **Explain the relationship between hard work and success.**

Work with a Purpose

Those who work skillfully and efficiently have a purpose. They see the value of their work, whether it is at school where their grades are good or at a job where their customers are happy. Good workers are also wise. ❺ They gather during the summer, which means they make the most of times of plenty and look ahead to times of want (Prov. 10:5). A prosperous time is not the time to rest but the time to prepare for the future.

❺ **What does it mean to gather in the summer?**

❻ Sometimes it is easier not to try something that is hard. You might need to get a tutor for the Spanish class you are struggling with. You may need to get a part-time job to pay for gas in your car. You might even need to baby-sit your brother and sister when your parents ask you to. The truth is that you won't recognize a gain without extra effort. Solomon explains that even though a farmer has to feed and clean up after oxen, he wouldn't have much of a crop without them (Prov. 14:4).

❻ **What does Proverbs 14:4 mean about oxen and a harvest?**

Work with a Plan

Without a plan, hard work can be wasted effort. To be more efficient, we must work smarter, not harder. Proverbs says that when you build a house, you must first prepare the ground and the field where you will plant your crop (Prov. 24:27). **❼** In other words, have your future sustainable and your preparations made before you worry about comfort. Who wants to begin the process of building a science fair project only to run out of materials when the store is closed and the project is due the next day? The Bible describes someone who sets out to build a tower and runs out of money as someone who fails to plan (Luke 14:28-30).

❼ What does Proverbs 24:27 mean about first preparing the ground and then building the house?

A Hard-Work Attitude

For some people, laziness is an attitude. A lazy person's motto is, "If it isn't broken, don't fix it." Solomon gives the example of a lazy person who puts no effort into cooking his game (Prov. 12:27). Why would you work hard to kill the game and then not care about how you cook it?

❽ By contrast, hard workers take care of their possessions. They put in extra effort to keep their school supplies neat, their cars repaired, and their future bright. Many times those who plan and take care of their things are ridiculed for their actions. They are mocked because they keep track of things like pens, pencils, and notebooks at school. They're made fun of because they clean their rooms regularly. Many times teenagers have a difficult time respecting the hard work of others. This lazy attitude is their enemy. It will not save them from stress or work and will only make matters worse in the end.

❽ Give some examples of how hard workers take care of their things.

Distracting Addictions

Self-control is related to laziness. A love of comfort rather than a desire for work leads many people into a me-centered life that ensnares them in addictions. Addictions come in many forms. Some people are addicted to the Internet, coffee, drugs, and alcohol. Once their addiction consumes them, they become lazy in other areas of their life as well. Addictions become wasteful habits.

Peers often gossip about a teenager with an addiction to alcohol, drugs, or pornography. However, an addiction to entertainment, parties, or anything non-productive can be just as bad. **❾** Addiction is a cruel ruler. It distracts us from our purpose in life as it promises pleasure, rest, and freedom but delivers misery, stress, and bondage. Hard work and balance are the wiser course.

❾ Describe how addiction is a cruel ruler.

SMALL-GROUP TIME:
Use this time to help students begin to integrate the truth they've learned into their lives while they connect with the other students in the group, the leaders, and with God.

After presenting the teaching material, ask students to divide back into small groups and discuss the "Do What?" questions. Small group facilitators should lead the discussions and set they tone by being open and honest in responding to each question.

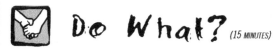

Do What? *(15 MINUTES)*

1. What is the hardest job you've ever done? What made that job so difficult? How did you feel when you finished it?

2. How do you honestly feel about school? Check one.
   - ☐ I love it!
   - ☐ I like the friends I have at school.
   - ☐ I look for any excuse to miss.
   - ☐ I'd rather sleep all day than go.
   - ☐ I would enjoy it more if I got paid.
   - ☐ School isn't fun, but at least I'm learning something I can use later in life.
   - ☐ Other:_____

3. How motivated are you at school? Check one.
   - ☐ I'm more addicted to video games and entertainment than school.
   - ☐ I hit the snooze button four or five times before dragging myself out of bed.
   - ☐ After some caffeine, I'm ready to hit it hard.
   - ☐ I don't mind it, but I wish others would have a better attitude.
   - ☐ I would drop out if I could find a way to survive.
   - ☐ I'm satisfied and enjoy getting an education.
   - ☐ Other:_____

4. Which areas of your life do you need to commit to hard work? How hard do you work at your spiritual life? Why should you work on your spiritual life at all?

5. What can help someone who is addicted, whether it be to a substance or a behavior? Have you ever been affected by someone with an addiction? How has that affected your view of that substance or behavior?

LifePoint Review

Everyone can use a little more self-control and hard work in their lives. Laziness leads to boredom. God advises us to have self-control and work hard in life.

"Do" Points:

These "Do" Points will help you grab hold of this week's LifePoint. Risk being open and honest as you answer the questions within your small group.

1. <u>Commit to work hard in all you do.</u> Look for opportunities to learn and grow.
   On what will you work hard this week? How?

2. <u>Search your life for distracting addictions.</u> You might not be addicted to pornography, alcohol, or drugs, but you may spend more time watching television than you should. Honestly evaluate your habits and identify your addictions.
   To what are you addicted? How do these addiction distract you from hard work?

3. <u>Recognize laziness in your life.</u> There is nothing wrong with relaxing, but when you spend more time relaxing than working, you become lazy.
   Do your lazy times outweigh your active times? What can you do to become more active?

Prayer Connection:

This is the time to encourage, support, and pray for each other in our journeys to trust God and seek out real and personal encounters with Him.

Share prayer needs with the group, especially those related to hearing from and responding to God. Your group facilitator will close your time in prayer.

Prayer Needs:

 # now What?

Deepen your understanding of who God is and continue the journey you've begun today by choosing one of the following assignments to complete this week:

Option 1:

Pick an area of your life that you are not devoting enough attention to, and focus on it this week. For example, if it is school or chores, spend less time than normal on the computer, phone, or with friends to make up the time. As you focus on the neglected area, pray for God to give you the proper attitude about its importance. Journal about what you discover about yourself and the benefits or negatives of working hard.

Option 2:

Everyone has distractions that stand in the way of productivity. Prayerfully identify that "thing" that distracts you from being your best. It may be television or the computer, or it may be electronic games or idle time on the phone. Take this into consideration and begin a "Stop Doing" list. This may not mean cutting out something entirely, instead it may mean spending half of the time you currently use. Bring your "Stop Doing" list next week.

Bible Reference notes

Use these notes to deepen your understanding as you study the Bible on your own:

Proverbs 10:4 — *poor.* In Proverbs, poverty is usually associated with laziness or a lack of discipline.

Proverbs 10:5 — *harvest.* Solomon's culture was agricultural. He often uses the image of harvest to illustrate a person who understands the discipline of taking care of himself. In chapter 6 he used the hard-working ant to make the same comparison (6:6-8).

Proverbs 12:27 — *roast.* This may refer to the preparation of food or to preparation for the hunt. The point is that the lazy person doesn't adequately provide for himself and his family.

Proverbs 20:1 — *Wine . . . beer.* Wine here refers to fermented grape juice. Beer was made from barley, dates, or pomegranates. Priests were forbidden to drink beer because it was so intoxicating.

Proverbs 24:27 — *afterwards, build your house.* Since the culture was agrarian, the first priority was establishing the land and planting the seed. After that the people could build houses and establish families.

Session

12

THE EMOTIONAL ROLLER COASTER

Connections Prep

MAIN LIFEPOINT: Our emotions are powerful. We can be paralyzed by fear and depression or ecstatic because of a good memory or a joyful experience. In order to become truly wise, we must learn to understand our emotions.

To reinforce the LifePoint, leaders and small-group facilitators should understand the following more detailed CheckPoints and "Do" Points.

BIBLE STUDY CHECKPOINTS:
- Recognize the power of emotions
- Learn how to help people who are sad or depressed
- Understand the definition of true joy

LIFE CHANGE "DO" POINTS:
- Encourage someone who is depressed or sad
- Recognize the emotions of others
- Commit to be honest about your emotions

PREPARATION:
☐ Review the leader book for this session and prepare your teaching.
☐ Determine how you will subdivide students into small discussion groups.
☐ Recruit mature students or adults as small-group facilitators. Be sure these facilitators plan to attend.

REQUIRED SUPPLIES:
☐ *Proverbs: Uncommon Sense* leader books for each group facilitator
☐ *Proverbs: Uncommon Sense* student books for each student
☐ Pens or pencils for each student

This "Get Ready" section is primarily for the students, but leaders and facilitators will benefit from these devotionals as well.

Read one of these short Bible passages each day and spend a few minutes wrapping your brain around it. Be sure to jot down any insights you discover.

MONDAY

Read Proverbs 14:10.

What makes your heart bitter? What makes you excited? When was the last time you were genuinely excited? How did you act? Did you care who was watching your reaction?

TUESDAY

Read Proverbs 14:13.

Have you ever put on a smile when you were sad? Why? How did you feel afterward?

WEDNESDAY

Read Proverbs 14:30.

Would you rather be peaceful or stressful? Why? How does stress affect you? Do others notice when you are stressed? What do they say to you?

THURSDAY

Read Proverbs 15:13.

How hard is it for people to know your emotions? Do you try to hide your emotions or do you let others see how you truly feel?

FRIDAY

Read Proverbs 15:30.

Who is the most cheerful person you know? Why is he or she so cheerful? How important is it to you to share a laugh with your friends and family? What have you done in the past that always makes you smile when you think about it?

SATURDAY

Read Proverbs 18:14.

Which is worse, being physically sick or depressed? Have you ever been depressed? What caused your depression?

SUNDAY

Read Proverbs 25:20.

How can you best help someone who is hurting? What do you think this passage is telling you?

LARGE-GROUP OPENING:
Get everyone's attention. Make announcements. Open your session with a prayer. Read the LifePoint to the students.

Ask if anyone brought a "Stop Doing" list from Option 2 out of the "Now What?" activities.

 LifePoint

Our emotions are powerful. We can be paralyzed by fear and depression or ecstatic because of a good memory or a joyful experience. In order to become truly wise, we must learn to understand our emotions.

12

SMALL-GROUP TIME:
Instruct students to
separate into smaller
groups of 4-8,
preferably in a circle
configuration. Call on
the mature student
or adult leaders you
recruited to facilitate
each small group
through this "Say
What?" segment.

Say What? *(15 MINUTES)*

Random Question of the Week:
Should vegetarians eat animal crackers?

Group Experience: Baby If You Love Me . . .

Play a round of "If you love me, SMILE" with the students in your small group. Have students put on a rigid face—no smiling allowed. Then look at each student one by one and say, "Baby if you love me, SMILE!" Be as creative and dramatic as you can when you speak to each student. Whoever does not smile within 10 seconds receives one point. Continue until each student has had the opportunity to try to make others smile. This provides some hilarious reactions and allows many people to prove their ability to remain stone-faced in the most laughable circumstances.

When you have finished the activity, ask the following questions:

1. Which was more difficult, trying to keep a straight face or trying to make others laugh? Why? How did you try to keep your face from smiling? Did you have a hard time not expressing on the outside what you were feeling on the inside? Why?

2. What is the craziest thing you have ever done because you were "caught up in the moment"? What were the results?

3. What past event has made you the happiest? What has made you the saddest? Do your emotions ever get the best of you? Describe a time when you were emotional and didn't hide it.

LARGE-GROUP TIME:
Have the students turn
to face the front for
this teaching time. Be
sure you can make
eye contact with each
student in the room.
Encourage students to
follow along and take
notes in their student
books.

So What? *(30 MINUTES)*

Teaching Outline

I. The Power of Emotions
    A. Emotions are powerful

    B. Emotions make us great, but they can also make us weak

    C. To understand people is to understand emotion

II. Proverbs 14:10,13,30; 15:13,30; 18:14; 25:20

III. An Emotional King
    A. King David experienced a range of emotions

    B. Some people are good at hiding their emotions

    C. We must learn to recognize their pain and discomfort

IV. Emotions and Health
    A. Emotions affect us physically

    B. To be successful at life, we must be able to read people and understand
       their reactions

V. Emotions Are Personal and Real
    A. Your emotions are real

    B. Depressed people need encouragement

    C. Empathy helps us relate to others

VI. Hidden Emotions
    A. People hide emotions because they don't want others to know about a
       problem in their lives

    B. People hide their emotions because they are embarrassed to show
       emotion publicly

    C. Honesty leads to openness about emotions

VII. Changing Emotions
    A. You can't base your life on emotions

    B. Emotions are usually a response to circumstances

    C. God doesn't change when circumstances do

12

TEACHING FOR THE
LARGE GROUP:

As you share the
"So What?" information
with students, make
it your own. Use your
natural teaching style.
You may modify it with
your own perspectives
and teaching needs.
Emphasize the
underlined information,
which gives key points,
answers to the student
book questions or fill-in-
the-blanks in the (shown
in the margins).

❶ How do different
emotions affect us?

❷ Why are emotions
hard to see and
understand?

Before the session,
enlist a student to read
Proverbs 14:10,13,30;
15:13,30; 18:14;
25:20.

VIII. Influential Emotions
   A. Mere happiness is feeling good about a pleasant circumstance or pleasure
   B. True joy knows a kind of hope that never changes
   C. Interaction with people is largely about emotions

The Power of Emotions

Emotions are powerful. **❶** <u>Depression powerfully paralyzes us. Laughter lifts our spirits. Joy takes us to heights we seek again and again. We are moved by experiences like watching a good movie. We can sit in the rain for an incredible outdoor concert or fireworks show because of the emotions these experiences produce.</u>

Emotions make us great, but they can also make us weak. **❶** <u>Joy adds energy, and depression saps it. Hope motivates, and sadness deflates.</u> A lot of what we do, we do because of emotion.

To understand people is to understand emotion. **❷** <u>Yet, emotion is often hidden or restrained. We let our emotions show only around those we fully trust. If we have an outburst of emotion when we don't feel safe, we say we lost control.</u> We guard our true emotions because of our past experiences. Maybe you were corrected as a child for crying at an inappropriate time or were told to put on a "happy face" even though you didn't feel like it. Though they are at times invisible, emotions are a key to understanding why people do what they do.

Learning from the Bible

The heart knows its own bitterness,
and no outsider shares in its joy.–Proverbs 14:10

Even in laughter a heart may be sad,
and joy may end in grief.–Proverbs 14:13

A tranquil heart is life to the body,
but jealousy is rottenness to the bones.–Proverbs 14:30

A joyful heart makes a face cheerful,
but a sad heart produces a broken spirit.–Proverbs 15:13

Bright eyes cheer the heart;
good news strengthens the bones.–Proverbs 15:30

LARGE-GROUP TIME CONTINUED:
This is the meat of the teaching time. Remind students to follow along and take notes in their student books.

As you share the "So What?" information with students, make it your own. Use your natural teaching style. You may modify it with your own perspectives and teaching needs. Emphasize the underlined information which gives answers to the student book questions or fill-in-the-blanks in the (shown in the margins).

❸ How did David express his emotions?

A man's spirit can endure sickness,
but who can survive a broken spirit.—Proverbs 18:14

Singing songs to a troubled heart is
like taking off clothing on a cold day,
or like pouring vinegar on soda.—Proverbs 25:20

An Emotional King

King David is known as a man after God's own heart (1 Sam. 13:14). He experienced a range of emotions and expresses them throughout the Psalms. He was broken before God, and he delighted in God's protection and grace. ❸ David was frequently depressed and wrote many Psalms during stressful periods: "I am weary from my groaning; with my tears I dampen my pillow and drench my bed every night. My eyes are swollen from grief; they grow old because of all my enemies" (Ps. 6:6-7). When David was in exile in the desert running from Saul and later from his own son, Absalom, he was alone in his grief. He did not have his best friend, Jonathan, with him to be an encouragement. He prayed, and God kept his grief from overwhelming him. He prayed and was able to see hope in God. His depression did not heal instantly, but he was able to keep going. ❸ David was also joyful: "Lord, the king finds joy in Your strength. How greatly he rejoices in Your victory! You have given him his heart's desire and have not denied the request of his lips. For You meet him with rich blessings; You place a crown of pure gold on his head" (Ps. 21:1-3). He delighted to express his rejoicing, and he was obviously strengthened by his joy.

Emotions are intensely personal, universally important, and irresistibly powerful. Regardless of how well we can hide or contain our emotions, we must realize that everyone has them—some are just better at hiding them than others. Whether we choose to show our emotions or not is our choice, but we must learn that emotions are constantly present. When others ask, "What's wrong?" or "Are you OK?" our faces and our simple body language may be telling a story we don't want to reveal. When we see someone obviously hurting, even when they deny it, we must learn to recognize their pain and discomfort.

Emotions and Health

The world did not wait until the development of psychology to understand the effects emotions have on health and life. By Solomon's time, people already knew about the health effects of stress, depression, and hopelessness. People noticed that physical illness was related to a person's emotional state. In a similar way, people have always sought joy and happiness because of its relationship to health

12

and energy. From the wholesome joy of friends to the unwholesome search for happiness in sinful pursuits, humankind has always celebrated joy.

The hope that comes from joy affects us physically. It makes our faces glad (Prov. 15:13), gives health to our bodies (Prov. 14:30), strengthens our bones (Prov. 15:30), and sustains us when we are sick (Prov. 18:14). On the other hand, depression, grief, and hopelessness rots the bones, breaks the spirit, and makes it hard to survive, much less thrive. Stress causes heart problems and shortens life. Depression weakens the immune system. The physical effects of emotion are undeniable and medically proven.

Emotions Are Personal and Real

"The heart knows its own bitterness," Solomon said (Prov. 14:10). To those on the outside, a person's emotions may not seem real. If, for example, you are depressed about a friend excluding you from an activity, your dejection may seem exaggerated to some. To you, however, there is no exaggeration. The feeling of doom is very real.

❹ Why is it a mistake to underrate emotion?

❹ It is wrong to try to comfort a friend by saying, "What you're experiencing is no big deal." To him, you are actually saying, "Your sadness is not important." Depressed people want to be understood, and they want to have their sadness acknowledged. You won't be able to encourage when you are downplaying the reality of someone's grief. Yet, if it is a mistake to ignore or underrate other people's emotions, it is also a mistake to offer meaningless cheer. If you are not properly dressed in the cold, you will shiver and be uncomfortable. If you pour vinegar on soda, an eruption occurs. This is Solomon's analogy to someone who offers cheap encouragement to a depressed person (Prov. 25:20).

Part of what makes friends important is their ability to share joy. Outsiders don't share joy (Prov. 14:10). Close friends share in common a bond that makes one person's joy the other's. The ability to understand another's grief or share his joy is *empathy.* The word understanding is related to the word *empathy.* People are looking for empathy whether they realize it or not. This is why Paul said, "Rejoice with those who rejoice; weep with those who weep" (Rom. 12:15). If we are going to be people who help and heal others, we need to be able to empathize with others.

❺ What are two sources of encouragement?

A "don't worry, be happy" attitude is not sufficient; it makes for a fun song to sing, but makes for terrible friendship advice. ❺ True encouragement comes from two sources: empathy and hope. A depressed person needs understanding, not a casual dismissal of the reality of grief. He needs a reason to hope and believe that life will get better.

Hidden Emotion

It is not easy to be empathetic toward those around us because people hide their emotions. Solomon put it this way, "Even in laughter a heart may be sad" (Prov. 14:13). ❻ People hide emotions for two reasons. First, people hide emotions because they don't want others to know about a problem in their life. For example, a student whose parents are going through a nasty divorce doesn't want his friends to know. In public he puts on a face and smiles when he feels like crying. Secondly, people hide their emotions because they are embarrassed to show emotion publicly. Emotional people are often looked at as weak and fragile. Imagine walking through the hall of your school and seeing the most athletic person in your school crying. What would you think? You'd probably begin to categorize that person immediately.

The best way to help people who hide their emotions is to share honestly with them. If you are an honest friend who is open about your feelings, others will trust you. When you are honest with your emotions, you show others it is OK to be honest with their feelings as well.

Changing Emotions

In the days when sailing was the only way to cross large bodies of water, people could not always get where they wanted to go when they wanted to. If the prevailing winds were toward the coast, it would at times be impossible to make a journey. Staking your life on emotions is like staking your life on the wind. "Joy may end in grief," Solomon warns (Prov. 14:13). Emotions are usually a response to circumstances. When something good happens, we are happy. But when the good turns bad, so do our emotions. Circumstances shift and change along with our feelings, but there can and should be a better basis for joy than circumstance. That is why David spoke to God during his depression. God doesn't change with the circumstances.

Influential Emotions

There is a better way to cope with the changing winds of emotion. We can understand what joy and hope really are. ❼ Mere happiness is feeling good about a pleasant circumstance or pleasure. True joy knows a kind of hope that never changes. Solomon says, "The LORD will be your confidence and will keep your foot from a snare" (Prov. 3:26). True joy knows that something better awaits and that the troubles of now are not the end of the story.

❽ Wisdom includes knowing how people think and react in different situations. To be successful at life, we must be able to read people and understand their reactions. If you provoke an angry person, be ready for fireworks. If you try to ignore a person's sadness, get ready for bitterness. If you try to deflate the joy of others, be ready to be avoided. Interaction with people is largely about emotion.

❻ Why do people hide emotions?

❼ What is the difference between mere happiness and true joy?

❽ How is understanding emotion related to wisdom?

157

SMALL-GROUP TIME:
Use this time to help
students begin to
integrate the truth
they've learned into their
lives while they connect
with the other students
in the group, the
leaders, and with God.

After presenting the
teaching material, ask
students to divide back
into small groups and
discuss the "Do What?"
questions. Small group
facilitators should lead
the discussions and
set they tone by being
open and honest in
responding to each
question.

 # Do What? *(15 MINUTES)*

1. Is it easier for life to bring you joy or depression? Why? Who affects your emotions more than anyone else?

2. When you are depressed, how do you react? Can others tell how you feel, or do you try to hide your depression? Do you long to be around others to cheer you up, or do you avoid others?

3. When you are joyful, how do you react? Can others tell your emotion, or do you try to hide your feelings? Do you enjoy the company of others? Do you desire to spend time alone? What is one thing you like to do when you are joyful?

4. Describe a time when you were either joyful or depressed and reacted emotionally. Did you care how others viewed you? What eventually changed your emotion?

5. Complete this sentence, "When I am around my friends . . ." Check one.
   - ☐ I try to let them know what my honest emotions are.
   - ☐ I try to hide my true feelings because I want to fit in with everyone else.
   - ☐ I wear a mask everyday; I don't ever show my emotions.
   - ☐ We don't worry about each other's emotions.
     We all have problems and agree to not talk about them.
   - ☐ I don't care what they say about my emotions.
     If they can't accept me, I don't need them.
   - ☐ Other:

Small-group facilitators should reinforce the LifePoint for this session. Make sure that student's questions are invited and addressed honestly.

 # LifePoint Review

Our emotions are powerful. We can be paralyzed by fear and depression or ecstatic because of a good memory or a joyful experience. In order to become truly wise, we must learn to understand our emotions.

"Do" Points:

These "Do" Points will help you grab hold of this week's LifePoint. Be open and honest as you answer the questions within your small group.

1. Commit to be honest about your emotions. When you hide your emotions, you silently tell others that honesty isn't acceptable.
   Have you ever hidden your emotions? Why? Do you have friends who can handle the truth about your emotions?

2. Recognize the emotions of others. Be on the lookout for other's feelings.
   Do you think the people in your life are being honest about their emotions? When you encounter someone who is joyful, how do you react?

3. Encourage someone who is depressed or sad. When someone is sad or depressed, the last thing they need is a false sense of hope. Telling someone, "Everything is going to be fine" can sound insincere or cliche.
   How can you offer encouragement to someone who is going through a difficult time? Which is more important to someone who is hurting, your words or your time and effort?

12

Prayer Connection:

This is the time to encourage, support, and pray for each other in our journeys to trust God and seek out real and personal encounters with Him.

Share prayer needs with the group, especially those related to hearing from and responding to God. Your group facilitator will close your time in prayer.

Prayer Needs:

Be sure to end your session by asking students to share prayer needs with one another, especially as they relate to issues brought up by today's session.

Encourage students to list prayer needs for others in their books so they can pray for one another during the week. Assign a student coordinator in each small group to gather the group's requests and e-mail them to the group members.

 now What?

Encourage students to dig a little deeper by completing a "Now What?" assignment before the next time you meet. Remind students about the "Are You Ready?" short daily Bible readings and related questions at the beginning of session 13.

Deepen your understanding of who God is and continue the journey you've begun today by choosing one of the following assignments to complete this week:

Option 1:

Keep a journal of your emotions for the week. When are you uneasy, sad, or lonely? When are you elated, peaceful, or content? Are you alone or with friends at the time? What seems to be related to your joy or sadness? Is it a circumstance, an experience, or a thought?

Option 2:

Become a journalist and pretend you're writing a story on the power of emotions. Interview friends, family, and teachers or coaches. Take notes. Learn from them how emotions have helped them in their journeys, but also learn ways that emotions have perhaps gotten in the way or hurt them. Ask about specific memories that still resonate in the deep places. Be mindful to remember certain words of wisdom that are shared. What kind of story would you write when your interviews are complete? Come prepared next week to pitch your story idea to the editor.

Bible Reference Notes

Use these notes to deepen your understanding as you study the Bible on your own:

Proverbs 14:33   *laughter.* Laughter is good medicine for our souls. However, while it may relieve stress of a person who is suffering, it is only a temporary escape from the reality of struggles.

Proverbs 15:13   *sad heart.* Maintaining sadness in our hearts crushes our spirits, creating discouragement, disillusion, and hopelessness.

Proverbs 15:30   *Bright eyes.* This is the sparkle or gleam in the eyes when good news comes. *strengthens the bones.* This joy invigorates our body, mind, and spirt.

NOTES

Session

13

DON'T BE SILLY

Connections Prep

MAIN LIFEPOINT:

No matter who we are, how smart we are, or how much money we have, we probably continue to make the same mistakes over and over again. We must pursue wisdom in order to keep our lives sharp and our eyes open.

To reinforce the LifePoint, leaders and small-group facilitators should understand the following more detailed CheckPoints and "Do" Points.

BIBLE STUDY CHECKPOINTS:

· Realize how necessary wisdom is in our daily lives
· Understand the consequences of not learning from our mistakes
· Discover the importance of pursuing wisdom daily

LIFE CHANGE "DO" POINTS:

· Commit to search for wisdom
· List the important Proverbs and ideas that have helped you throughout this series
· Focus on listening to someone whom you don't listen to enough

PREPARATION:

☐ Review the leader book for this session and prepare your teaching.
☐ Determine how you will subdivide students into small discussion groups.
☐ Recruit mature students or adults as small-group facilitators. Be sure these facilitators plan to attend.
☐ With a poster board or tear sheet, designate one wall as the "True" wall and another as the "False" wall for the "Say What?" activity.

REQUIRED SUPPLIES:

☐ *Proverbs: Uncommon Sense* leader books for each group facilitator
☐ *Proverbs: Uncommon Sense* student books for each student
☐ Pens or pencils for each student

 Get Ready

Read one of these short Bible passages each day and spend a few minutes wrapping your brain around it. Be sure to jot down any insights you discover.

MONDAY

Read Proverbs 18:2.

Do you listen or talk more? Why? Which is better, to listen to understand or talk to hear your own voice?

TUESDAY

Read Proverbs 18:6.

Have you ever spoken words that led to conflict? Describe one time and its outcome.

WEDNESDAY

Read Proverbs 13:14; 19:8.

What are some snares that you have avoided because of the advice of someone else? Did you listen to their advice immediately, or did you have to see evidence that they knew what they were talking about? Explain.

THURSDAY

Read Proverbs 21:16; 27:12.

How can you stray away from wisdom? What are the effects of straying? How have you either escaped danger or suffered because you chose to listen to or ignore someone else's advice?

FRIDAY **Read Proverbs 10:19; 29:11,20.**

How important are your words? When was the last time your words got you in trouble? How did you reconcile with the person you offended? Was simply saying "I'm sorry" enough?

SATURDAY **Read Proverbs 11:12; 18:6.**

Have you ever been made fun of? How did you feel when others talked about you? Have you ever made fun of someone else? Why?

SUNDAY **Read Proverbs 24:3-4.**

Can you describe your life as a "well-built" house? How can your knowledge of wisdom found throughout this Proverbs study be a foundation for you to build on? What have you learned from this study that has affected you the most?

LARGE-GROUP OPENING:
Get everyone's attention. Make announcements. Open your session with a prayer. Read the LifePoint to the students.

Ask about the "Now What?" activity from session 12. Are there any journalists to pitch their stories?

 LifePoint

No matter who we are, how smart we are, or how much money we have, we probably continue to make the same mistakes over and over again. We must pursue wisdom in order to keep our lives sharp and our eyes open.

13

SMALL-GROUP TIME:
Call on the mature
student or adult
leaders you recruited
to facilitate each small
group through the "Say
What?" segment.

 # Say What? *(15 MINUTES)*

Random Question of the Week:
Why do doctors call what they do "practice"?

Group Experience: The Moving Quiz

Designate one wall in your meeting area as "True" and the opposite wall as "False." Tell students that you are going to give them a quiz, and they must go to the appropriate wall to "show" their answers. If they are correct, they are to remain standing, if they are incorrect, they are to sit down. The game is over when either everyone is seated, or when all the questions have been asked.

1. In the weightlessness of space a frozen pea will explode if it comes in contact with Pepsi. *(True)*
2. Johnny Plessey batted .331 for the Cleveland Spiders in 1891, even though he spent the entire season batting with a rolled-up, lacquered copy of *The Toledo Post-Dispatch. (True)*
3. The humpback whale is the largest animal in the world *(False—blue whale)*
4. Mount Kilimanjaro in Africa is the highest point in the world. *(False—Mount Everest)*
5. The Air Force's F-117 fighter uses aerodynamics discovered during research into how bumblebees fly. *(True)*
6. King Henry VIII slept with a gigantic axe. *(True)*
7. The Venezuelan brown bat can detect and dodge individual raindrops in mid-flight, arriving safely back at his cave completely dry. *(True)*
8. The average human has 66 birthdays *(False—only 1 day of birth!)*
9. Canada does not have a 4th of July *(False—it's right after the 3rd of July!)*
10. In 10 minutes, a hurricane releases more energy than all the world's nuclear weapons combined *(True)*

After the exercise, ask these follow-up questions:

1. Were any of these "facts" surprising to you? Which ones?

2. Describe the most foolish thing you have ever done. Why did you do it? Who were you with when you did it?

3. What is the wisest decision you have made lately? Why did you make that decision? Were the lessons on Proverbs helpful in you making your wise decision? Why or why not?

So What? *(30 MINUTES)*

LARGE-GROUP TIME:
Have the students turn to face the front for this teaching time. Be sure you can make eye contact with each student in the room. Encourage students to follow along and take notes in their student books.

Share the "So What?" information with your large group of students. You may modify it with your own perspectives and teaching needs. Be sure to highlight the underlined information, which gives answers to the student book questions and fill-in-the-blanks (shown in the margins).

Teaching Outline

I. Not as Easy as it Looks
A. In order to excel at something, you have to practice and learn how to participate in the activity
B. Wisdom, as with all godliness, is first learned in the mind and then carried out actively in your life

II. Proverbs 10:19; 11:12; 13:14; 18:2,6,15; 19:8; 21:16; 24:3-4; 27:12; 29:11,20

III. Wisdom Versus Foolishness
A. The wise are skilled at managing life's circumstances and experiences
B. The wise benefit from life's opportunities and avoid life's pitfalls
C. Being foolish is the opposite of being wise
D. The choice between wisdom and foolishness is a commitment to learn, listen, and grow

IV. Wisdom Preserves Life
A. Wisdom prevents disaster
B. Wisdom brings success

V. Foolishness Brings a Beating
A. Foolishness is comparable to a trap
B. The way of the fool is the way of death
C. God is the ultimate wisdom and knowing Him leads to life

VI. Wisdom Is Listening
A. To become wiser, we must listen more
B. Arguments result from not listening
C. People will trust you if you're a good listener

VII. Foolishness Is Speaking
A. In many cases, silence is the best policy
B. It is better to ask and learn than speak and show that you know nothing

VIII. Wisdom Builds a House

A. The teachings of God are the rock of wisdom

B. Build your family and your reputation with wisdom

C. The treasures that come from wisdom are much greater than silver and gold

Not as Easy as It Looks

Have you ever noticed that people who are good at something seem to come by it easily? You see a guitar player's fingers walking easily up and down the neck of a guitar, and you think, "That looks easy." Then you buy a book, attempt to learn guitar yourself, and discover how wrong you were. You can never become a star football player or a champion figure skater merely by watching from the side. In order to excel at something, you have to practice and learn how to participate in the activity. ❶ In the same way, wisdom is not as easy to obtain as it seems. When you see a person who calms conflict and exhibits self-control, you may be tempted to think it is his personality. We may call him laid back or even-tempered. The reality is he has wisdom.

❶ **How can wisdom seem deceptively easy?**

It is easier to know wisdom in your head than to practice it with your life. Yet, wisdom, as with all godliness, is first learned in the mind and then carried out actively in your life. ❷ To bring wisdom from the mind into action takes effort, rehearsal, and patience. You must make a conscious effort to let wisdom affect your actions as well as your thoughts.

❷ **What does it take to get wisdom not only in your head but also into your actions?**

Learning from the Bible

When there are many words, sin is unavoidable, but the one who controls his lips is wise.—Proverbs 10:19

Before the session, enlist a student to read Proverbs 10:19; 11:12; 13:14; 18:2,6,15; 19:8; 21:16; 24:3-4; 27:12; 29:11,20.

Whoever shows contempt for his neighbor lacks sense, but a man with understanding keeps silent.—Proverbs 11:12

A wise man's instruction is a fountain of life, turning people away from the snares of death.—Proverbs 13:14

A fool does not delight in understanding, but only wants to show off his opinions.—Proverbs 18:2

A fool's lips lead to strife,
and his mouth provokes a beating.–Proverbs 18:6

The mind of the discerning acquires knowledge,
and the ear of the wise seeks it.–Proverbs 18:15

The one who acquires good sense loves himself;
one who safeguards understanding finds success.–Proverbs 19:8

The man who strays from the way of wisdom
will come to rest
in the assembly of the departed spirits.–Proverbs 21:16

A house is built by wisdom,
and it is established by understanding;
by knowledge the rooms are filled
with every precious and beautiful treasure.–Proverbs 24:3-4

The sensible see danger and take cover;
the foolish keep going and are punished.–Proverbs 27:12

A fool gives full vent to his anger,
but a wise man holds it in check.–Proverbs 29:11

Do you see a man who speaks too soon?
There is more hope for a fool than for him.–Proverbs 29:20

Wisdom vs. Foolishness

Wisdom is different from knowledge. In the Bible, knowledge is used to build skill at a trade or craft (Ex. 31:3-5). When you are wise in life, you are skilled at managing life's circumstances and experiences. The wise person benefits from life's opportunities and avoids life's pitfalls.

Foolishness is the opposite of wisdom. To be foolish is to live according to emotions and pride. If you follow your selfish nature, you will definitely face the consequences. ❸ You will have fewer friends and your relationships will be strained. Stress and conflict will be common, and money will fly out of your hands. God's way will seem an unconquerable mystery to you. Talking and passing notes in the back row of life's classroom is not an option for the person who is searching for wisdom. Wise people are found absorbing helpful insight in the front row.

❸ What are common consequences of living foolishly?

169

Some of the most interesting proverbs in Solomon's collection are about the contrast between wisdom and foolishness. Solomon writes over 40 times about a fool. "A fool's way is right in his own eyes, but whoever listens to counsel is wise" (Prov. 12:15). Considering that the book of Proverbs is some of the best counsel out there anywhere, it is fair to say that anyone who ignores it is a fool. Yet, whoever listens to Proverbs is wise. The choice between wisdom and foolishness is a commitment to learn, listen, and grow.

Wisdom Preserves Life

❹ How is wisdom a "fountain of life"?

Following wisdom preserves us from death—sometimes literally. Wisdom prevents disaster and brings success. ❹ Solomon says wisdom is a "fountain of life" (Prov. 13:14). The picture he gives is not of a fancy fountain in a city square but of a spring that brings water to a village. The spring is literally life in the dead desert. The difference is the living water (John 4:10-11), not the fountain. The inside is what ultimately counts. According to Solomon, the one who finds wisdom finds success (Prov. 19:8).

Foolishness Brings a Beating

If wisdom is a fountain of life, ignoring wisdom is quicksand. Foolishness is comparable to a trap (Prov. 13:14). Similarly, the fool who is quick to speak invites a beating (Prov. 18:6). This beating may be a literal one or some other consequence that the fool often has no idea what he did to deserve. "I'm just doing what everyone else does and saying what everyone else wants to say," the fool excuses himself. "Why should I be singled out?"

❺ How can foolishness be so devastating?

❺ The way of the fool is the way of death (Prov. 21:16). The ultimate foolishness is sin, which, without the grace of God, does lead to death. God is the ultimate wisdom and knowing Him leads to life. The fool, however, doesn't see punishment coming, including the coming judgment day of God. He keeps going in the same direction and is eventually punished for it (Prov. 27:12).

Wisdom Is Listening

❻ In addition to reading from Proverbs, what is another godly source of wisdom, according to Solomon?

❻ A large part of Solomon's wisdom involves listening. He mentions listening more than 10 times in the book of Proverbs. "The ear of the wise" seeks knowledge (Prov. 18:15). "A fool does not delight in understanding," which means a wise man does seek to understand (Prov. 18:2). The wise ear listens to criticism (Prov. 15:31) and to instruction (Prov. 28:9).

To become wiser we must listen more. We rarely give full attention to what someone else is saying in a conversation—even when our closest friends talk. One reason is that we are attempting to do too many things. We might be attempting to listen, sending an instant message, text messaging someone else, and planning where to go this weekend all at the same time. However, wisdom says, "The one who gives an answer before he listens—this is foolishness and disgrace for him" (Prov. 18:13). A lot of arguments result from not listening. Parents say their children don't listen to their advice and instruction. A friend or classmate becomes angry when you make a mistake because you did not listen when you should have.

Listening is not only important for relationships, but it is also important for gaining wisdom itself. Not only will you please your family and friends by hearing what they say, but you will also become wiser. A lot of wisdom is passed on by word of mouth and by hearing people's experiences. Someone tells you about a great cheap clothing store she has found. Bored, you almost don't hear a word she says. Then you find you need new clothes and wish you knew a good place to find some at a good price. The coach tells you about his experience against a rival team. During the game, you wish you'd listened more when the coach talked. "The ear of the wise" is always busy listening for information and wisdom from the experiences of others. Others will trust you if you are a good listener. The benefits of listening are undeniable.

Foolishness is Speaking

❼ If listening is a mark of the wise, speaking hastily is the typical mark of the fool: "When there are many words, sin is unavoidable, but the one who controls his lips is wise" (Prov. 10:19). If you keep your mouth open long enough, you're likely to put your foot in it.

In many cases, silence is the best policy. People sometimes anger you with their words or actions. Your temptation is to vent and talk about them. In the process, you gossip about someone else. "A man with understanding keeps silent," Solomon says (Prov. 11:12). No one will be angry with you for not gossiping and grumbling about others. But "a fool gives full vent to his anger" anyway (Prov. 29:11).

A fool "only wants to show off his opinions" (Prov. 18:2). This is another trap of being too quick to speak. No one really respects someone who is always expressing strong opinions with little information to back them up. It is better to ask and learn than speak and show that you know nothing.

Listening is wise. Speaking is often the vehicle to trouble. James says, "Everyone must be quick to hear, slow to speak" (Jas. 1:19). This is a habit worth cultivating. After all, there is more hope for a fool than someone who speaks too soon. (See Prov. 29:20.)

❼ If listening is crucial to having wisdom, how do the words you speak reflect that wisdom?

13

Wisdom Builds a House

Jesus says, "Everyone who hears these words of Mine and acts on them will be like a sensible man who built his house on the rock. The rain fell, the rivers rose, and the winds blew and pounded that house. Yet it didn't collapse, because its foundation was on the rock" (Matt. 7:24-25). ❽ <u>Jesus probably had Proverbs 24:3-4 in mind when He spoke of a house built on a rock. The teachings of God are the rock of wisdom. You will build your family and your reputation more with wisdom than you will by cheating, backstabbing, or gossiping about others.</u>

Honesty, integrity, and sound relationships with people will build lasting success that pleases God. The treasures that come from wisdom are much greater than silver and gold. A home filled with family and love is better than any mansion filled with conflict and resentment.

❽ Jesus talks about building the foundation on a rock. What rock do you think He is talking about?

Do What? *(15 MINUTES)*

SMALL-GROUP TIME: Use this time to help students begin to integrate the truth they've learned into their lives while they connect with the other students in the group, the leaders, and with God.

After presenting the teaching material, ask students to divide back into small groups and discuss the "Do What?" questions. Small group facilitators should lead the discussions and set they tone by being open and honest in responding to each question.

1. What is the most foolish action you have seen done in public? How did you feel when you saw it? Have you ever made a mistake like that?

2. What is the hardest part about being wise? Check one.
   - ☐ My past mistakes keep creeping back into my life.
   - ☐ I don't take the time to study Proverbs and learn how to be wise.
   - ☐ My friends don't care about wisdom.
   - ☐ I get busy, and I don't think about making wise choices.
   - ☐ I'm still young; I've got plenty of time to learn how to be wise.
   - ☐ I focus on making myself happy "NOW" rather than thinking about my future.

3. If you could gain wisdom in one specific area of your life, which area would it be? Why?

4. Do you believe God really cares about your choices? What choices does God leave up to you?

5. How can wisdom really change your life?

 # LifePoint Review

Small-group facilitators should reinforce the LifePoint for this session. Make sure that student's questions are invited and addressed honestly.

No matter who we are, how smart we are, or how much money we have, we probably continue to make the same mistakes over and over again. We must pursue wisdom in order to keep our lives sharp and our eyes open.

"Do" Points:

1. <u>Commit to search for wisdom.</u> The more wisdom you gain, the more your life will change.
   How can you begin your search for wisdom? Where do you need to start?

2. List the important Proverbs and ideas that have helped you throughout this series. Review what you have learned. Write notes about how you have been able to apply the wisdom you have gained.
   What can wisdom do for you?

3. Focus on listening to someone whom you don't listen to enough. Plan a time with this person just to listen and learn. When he is speaking, look him in the eye and focus. Ask questions. Try to understand what he is saying and why it is important to him. Afterwards, ask yourself, "Did I get to know him a little better just from trying harder to listen this one time?"
   How can being a better listener give you more opportunities to gain wisdom?

Be sure to end your session by asking students to share prayer needs with one another, especially as they relate to issues brought up by today's session.

Encourage students to list prayer needs for others in their books so they can pray for one another during the week. Assign a student coordinator in each small group to gather the group's requests and e-mail them to the group members.

Prayer Connection:

This is the time to encourage, support, and pray for each other in our journeys to trust God and seek out real and personal encounters with Him.

Share prayer needs with the group, especially those related to hearing from and responding to God. Your group facilitator will close your time in prayer.

Prayer Needs:

13

now What?

Deepen your understanding of what wisdom truly means to us, and continue the journey you've begun today by choosing one of the following assignments to complete this week:

Option 1:

List the Proverbs and ideas that have helped you throughout this study. Review the verses you previously memorized. Write notes about ways you have been able to apply that wisdom to your life.

Option 2:

Meditate on and memorize Proverbs 18:15. Meditating means repeating the verse over and over again and thinking about its meaning and applications. Ask yourself questions like: Am I in the habit of learning and observing? How can I live a better life today? You can aid memorization by writing the verse on an index card and putting it where you can see it. Work on the verse daily for at least a week

Bible Reference notes

Use these notes to deepen your understanding as you study the Bible on your own:

Proverbs 11:12   *shows contempt.* This refers to despising or belittling.

Proverbs 13:14   *instruction.* This is any kind of teaching or training.
fountain of life. This refers to the source of spiritual vitality and true fulfillment.

Proverbs 24:3-4   *house.* Any house, whether individual or family, is grounded in wisdom, strengthened by understanding, and prospered by knowledge.

Acknowledgments:

We sincerely appreciate the great team of people who worked to develop *Proverbs: Uncommon Sense, Youth Edition.* Special thanks are extended to Derek Leman for the content he composed for the adult version to which we are so indebted. Appreciation is also extended to Mike Wilson for writing the youth edition. We also appreciate the editorial and production team that consisted of Brian Daniel, Joe Moore of Powell Creative, Lori Mayes, and Sarah Hogg.

NOTES

GROUP DIRECTORY

PASS THIS DIRECTORY AROUND AND HAVE YOUR GROUP
MEMBERS FILL IN THEIR NAMES AND PHONE NUMBERS.

NAME	PHONE	E-MAIL